LYNCHING BARACK OBAMA

How Whites Tried to String Up the President

MOLEFI KETE ASANTE

Universal Write Publications LLC

No part of this publication may be reproduced in whole or in part, or stored in a retrieval system, or transmitted in any form or by any means, electronic, mechanical, photocopying, recording or otherwise, without written permission from the publisher, except in the case of newspapers, magazines and websites using quotations embodied in critical essays and reviews.

Lynchng Barack Obama: How Whites Tried to String Up the President

Copyright © 2016 Universal Write Publications LLC
All rights reserved.

For information:
For information email AdvisoryBoard@universalwrite.com
Website at www.UniversalWrite.com
Publisher: Universal Write Publications LLC

Mailing/Submissions
Universal Write Publications LLC
237 Flatbush Avenue, Suite 107
Brooklyn, NY 11217-5224

ISBN-10: 0-9825327-1-7
ISBN-13: 978-0-9825327-1-3

Contents

Preface by Ayo Sekai Rosier . . . . *v*

CHAPTER ONE: Spinning Chaos out of Democracy 1
CHAPTER TWO: The Rise of Racial Hostility. 31
CHAPTER THREE: The Symbol of Mass Hope 61
CHAPTER FOUR: The Cradle of Abiding Fear 73
CHAPTER FIVE: Denial of Authenticity 93
CHAPTER SIX: Demanding Guilt. 111
CHAPTER SEVEN: The Haunting Image of Meanness 119

PREFACE

Up until President Barack Obama was elected in 2008 as the first Black President of the United States of America, stereotypes and racism were considered past history. However, as Molefi Kete Asante demonstrates racism still permeates every sector of the society and the attacks on Barack Obama as President show how deeply many white Americans held to racist beliefs and actions.

It is one thing when we discuss racism and discrimination in movies, music videos, award shows like the Oscars, and news media and big theatre. It is altogether a totally different phenomenon when one sees how entrenched racism is on the national and international stage. In the White House, the seat of the most powerful human on earth, the President of the United States, who is also one of the most respected leader in the free world, has all of the symbols of the nation's presidency, the oval office, the East Room, the Rose Garden, and can fly on the presidential jet at will. For many whites this was the unthinkable, even in this enlightened age. The potential of Obama's election to the presidency and indeed the reality of his achievement as President stirred the sinister motives of many whites. Everything Obama did, said, and even whether or not he was born in the United States was questioned, denied, argued, and contested.

Asante's insightful exposé is based on what has been reported in the mass media by news reporters across the country that repeat various negative remarks made toward the president. Most vile and obscene have been some of the taunts of Tea Party members. They have used terms like "Ni**er," 'Fa**ot' shouted at the top of their voices or whispered on radio programs against the President. (Sam Stein, 2010 *Huffington Post*). In fact, *Politics365* noted in their research "The 10 Worst Moments of Disrespect towards President Obama" that Obama was highly disrespected in his role as campaigner and president. The author of the January 2012 article, also reminded us of moments such as when Governor Jan Brewer (R-AZ) decided to conduct business with the President in front of reporters, pointing her finger in his face as if scolding a child; and when a member of Congress watching a U.S. President during a joint session on live national television decided to shout **"*You lie!*," they appeared to be expressing their frustration that a black man was running the country.** Throughout President Obama's first term, the news media consistently refused to refer to Barack Obama as President Obama and the language would range between *Mr. Obama, simply Obama,* or *Barack Obama.* The presumption that anyone, especially, fellow politicians and news reporters on the national stage could call the president out of his name in many instances and circumstances have caused some to coin the first Black man of the free world *The Most Disrespected President in History* (*Daily Kos*, Aug, 2013).

The lens and frame through which most countries make judgments and determination about values tend to be the media. I wish to point out that Asante's essay on Obama's critics is largely based on mass media sources. The limited Media Effect Theory explains how and what we do both on the macro and the micro levels of society. Asante is seeking to point out that if the President of the United States of America can be humiliated in headlines such as Craig Steiner's *Common Sense American Conservatism* article entitled "Netanyahu schools Obama" (May, 2011) and *The Hill's* headline about how "Putin Snubs Obama" (Pecquet, 2012) those headlines show much more about the nation's search for negativity than they do about Obama's character. We worry about Black boys and girls being killed by a non-black American who shoots and kills a teenager at a gas station because he didn't like the music playing that was too loud (*New York Daily News*: Caulfield, 2012). And let's not forget Trayvon Martin (Alvarez, Buckley, 2013) who was killed by George Zimmerman supposedly because he did not like how he looked. Then there was the deaths of Michael Brown shot down in the streets of Ferguson, Missouri, and Eric Garner who died in the Staten Island chokehold, although caught on camera, produced no convictions of the police officers who killed them despite protest and outrage (Goodman, Baker 2014).

It is laughable to think that racism does not exist, or that it is in the past, or that there is anything near equality and justice in this country when these events have become too commonplace in our country and our culture. The mere fact that the *New Yorker* could show cartoon images of police officers shooting monkeys while making crude remarks about President Barack Obama, and derogatory suggestions towards Black people (Stein, 2009).

Why would anyone want to respect the first black President given the assaults on his office and his personal character? We can agree with Molefi Kete Asante that racism is so pervasive and prevalent, that many Americans see it as normal when in fact it should be considered pathological, sick, and insane behavior.

Asante takes up the issue of the attacks on the First Lady, Michelle Obama, as a part of the entire Obama assault narrative. Not only was the First Lady heckled but her children have been blasted as "lazy" and "disrespectful" for living in the White House. Elizabeth Lauten, an aide for a Republican Senator, but who also had a teenage prison record, according to *The Smoking Gun*, felt free enough and embolden enough to attack the president's children.

Clearly this book by Molefi Kete Asante underscores the fact that racism is not disappearing despite the wish that the nation had reached a post-racial reality after the election of Barack Obama. Racism is not disappearing. I salute the author of this important portrayal of the American society's most unimpressive underside.

Denise Ayo Sekai Rosier

CHAPTER ONE

Spinning Chaos Out of Democracy

Rudy Giuliani, former Mayor of New York City and a leading Republican politician said on February 19, 2015, "The President does not love America. He was not brought up the way you and I were brought up to love this country." The fact that Giuliani's comments came during the lead up to a nominating campaign for the 2016 election caused anxiety among many Republicans.

Only Senator Rand Paul stepped forward to say that he thought Giuliani was out of bounds. The other Republican candidates cowed like chicken refusing to come out of the outhouse to denounce Giuliani.

The United States is a liberal democracy. Its government depends upon the executive, legislative and judicial branches. Each branch has its own duties and obligations. However, the executive which includes the President of the United States and cabinet secretaries represents the single most visible aspect of the American government. This is so despite the implicit notion of the equality of the branches. Whoever occupies the position of president is considered the leader of the nation. However, since the United States is a liberal democracy there are various political parties and factions. The political Right-Wing is usually associated with the Republican Party. The Right-Wing opposes most forms of social democracy and rejects all calls for social ownership and social control of the means of production. In recent political history the American Right-Wing groups have included conservatives, Christian democrats, classical liberals, some ultra-nationalists and, at the extreme Right, there are people who may be called racists and fascists.

Conservative pundit Dinesh D'Souza, tweeted around the same time as Giuliani's comment about the President that "You can take the boy out of the ghetto, but...." February 18, 2015. D'Souza has often paraded a narrow nihilistic view of reality. His attack on Obama was not different from his generalized attacks on African Americans in during the 1990s when he and I debated on several occasions. He was then, and of course, later, a person who had limited knowledge and understanding of American history, which in my opinion is the source of most ignorance when it comes to politics. Indeed, D'Souza's Indian origin belied the fact that he was also a strong opponent of rights for the Dalits, the so-called Untouchables in India. His attack on Obama represents a strand of anti-liberalism that often becomes *ad hominem* assaults on the president.

The verbal abuse heaped upon President Obama and his family is akin to lynching, the American extrajudicial practice of executing someone accused of wrongdoing or someone believed to be exhibiting the wrong sensibilities, or someone who seems to lack the proper respect for white privilege. The lynch mob during the 19th and 20th centuries was an informal group of whites that took it upon themselves to chastise "uppity" blacks that thought they could participate in government, vote, speak freely, and exercise the rights given by the US Constitution.

An accused black person would typically not know his accusers and would not know the nature of his alleged crime until the law enforcement officers delivered him to the clutches of the mob. Of course, in most of the cases the crime was blackness itself, although blacks were accused of violent crimes such as rape and murder as well as violations of southern white mores that dictated that blacks should not walk on the sidewalks, for instance. During the nadir of race relations in the United States at the turn of the 20th century, Africans were lynched because whites feared the rise of black political power that had emerged during the 1870s and lasted for thirty to forty years. They were committed to the idea that blacks could not have political power over whites; to them this condition was literally unnatural, so twisted were their minds by the doctrine of racial superiority.

Emotional reactions to the Presidency of Barack Obama were reminiscent of the vile and obscene behavior of whites that could not bear to compete with blacks or have blacks in positions of authority over whites. Their reactions were systemic like an organism seeking to expel what it sees and feels as a "foreign" element. This is the context of all physical lynching in American history; whites whose emotional reactions to blacks were almost inhumanly physiological.

There was always strength in numbers and the lynch mob's energy often fed on the swelling crowds that came out to see the brutal spectacle of black bodies hanging in the wind. The stately live oak trees in the South saw many black bodies swinging like Spanish moss because of the evil assaults on blacks. Even children were brought to the occasions just to initiate them in the ugly business of lynching a black man. Of course, the aim was to intimidate the African masses; to weaken the will of black people to fight for civil and human rights, but countless numbers of black men and women kept rising to defend black dignity.

Most of those who became parts of lynch mobs never knew their victims, had never voted for a black man, and did not consider African Americans to be "real" Americans. In effect, the fact that they had defined Africans as being outside of the category of American meant that the person so defined could be harassed, maimed or killed. There did not have to be credible evidence of wrongdoing, just the proclamation by whites that something wrong had been done by some black person, man or woman. The person would be hunted like an animal, and when caught, beaten, taken to a tree or another high place, hung by the neck, and sometime castrated for all to see the de-masculinizing of a black man. In some instances, the body would be burned and the family of the deceased called to come and retrieve the ruined corpse.

Any black person who sought to assert economic, social, or physical power was a target for assault. Among the violations of customs and attitudes were these:

- Blacks could not raise their voices when talking to whites.
- Blacks could not be on the sidewalk when whites were on the sidewalk.
- Blacks could not have social conversations with whites.
- Blacks could not have physical contact with whites.
- Blacks could not look whites in the eye when talking to them.

Needless to say these unwritten but heavily enforced codes had been developed as a new means of controlling Africans after the end of the Civil War. With the plantation system in shambles the whites struggled for more innovative ways of keeping blacks from having the opportunity to compete with them. Any black who achieved recognition by other blacks and some whites had to be considered an enemy of the black codes.

The campaigns and elections of Barack Obama proved to be challenging occasions for white bigots who during an earlier age would have called for the lynching of Obama

Barack Obama is one of the most liberal presidents in a practical sense in the history of the United States although those farther to his left frequently challenged him to pursue even more progressive policies. Yet he brought to the office a strong ethical sense of governance that was based in his commitment to service to the poor and needy, something that few other presidents had been able to sustain given the nature of the normal road to the rise to power in America. A heavy reliance on self-determination and self-help almost in opposition to society's role in assisting the poor and weak also caused many presidents to abandon the thought of "doing something" for the masses. In Obama's vision of society the rich should share through taxation with the poor; the government should protect the weak from the strong; and diplomacy is much more effective than warfare.

When one goes in search of the Obama persona or policies that created such enormous amount of bitterness one inevitably discovers race. Although Obama's political ideology was contrary to that of the Republicans they challenged him on both personal and policy grounds but the coalescence seemed to always be around the issue of his race. While it was true in some instances that the assaults on him were personal when it came to race most of the attacks against him appeared to have something to do with the symbolic nature of his presidency, not even the substantive policies which he championed. If the attacks came on the policies it was because they were seen as favoring the poor and often blacks. Interestingly blacks liked Obama from the very beginning but there was a general belief that his election could bring out the worst in white people. During Obama's final years in office the assaults on him were often directed toward the generalized black community as some whites felt that they had lost the country and had to win or take the country from blacks at all costs. In fact, the mass murderer, Dylann Roof, who killed nine African Americans in a Charleston AME Church in 2015, claimed that blacks "rape our women and have taken over our country." This was clearly misguided because Obama did not produce the fear and trepidation that the young white Charleston killer felt although Obama's election and presidency may have created a sense of powerlessness in some whites.

While some whites took out their frustrations on black people in various capacities, whether as police officers, judges, probation officers, managers of stores, insurance executive, business partners, or teachers, African Americans generally reported that they felt more bitterness from whites during Obama's presidency. Even with this bitterness against black people in general whites kept up the negative racial attacks against Obama and his family.

Rodner Figueroa, a prominent commentator on Univision's show *El Gordo y La Flaca*, was dismissed for saying that Michelle Obama "looked like she is a part of the cast of *Planet of the Apes*" during one of his life segments in March 2015. There was immediate reaction to his comments and despite the fact that he was talking about Paolo Ballesteros' undertaking of transforming himself into several female celebrities.

In the early 1980s Black Consciousness was on the backburner and African Americans in the United States were losing ground in a distinctly specific drop-off from the period of intense awareness of the 1960s and 1970s. Black Power was gone, and the Civil Rights Struggle had become passé and had given way to a more urgent demand for liberation during the late 1970s and early 1980s. In 1982 Thomas Bradley, a former policeman, who had become long time mayor of Los Angeles ran for the governorship of California and most polls, had Bradley winning the governorship. When he lost the election it was obvious that white voters would say one thing and go into the voting booth and pull the lever for the white candidates. There is a generalized view that racist thinking and racist actions are acceptable to a wide spectrum of white America. The brilliant sociologist Joseph Feagin, author of Racist America, once told me that most whites believe that racism is normal. I think what he meant was that they did not see racism as something that suggested a psychological, social or mental illness. On the other hand, many African American psychologists such as Na'im Akbar,

Wade Nobles, and Frances Cress Welsing, see racism as a deviant response to other human beings. Daudi Azibo, a psychologist, pioneered an examination of why racism did not appear in the DSM.

In March 2015 when the Sigma Alpha Epsilon members were seen on a video singing a racist song that they had learned several years earlier while on a fraternity leadership cruise demonstrates how racism permeates the society. SAE was eventually kicked off the campus of the University of Oklahoma when the news got out that the racist song was part of a pledge process.

On March 8, 2015, President Boren of Oklahoma University asked the chapter to leave the campus. What do these two events: the Bradley campaign and the Oklahoma University fraternity have in common? I think that the work of Joseph Feagin, one of the key sociologists of race in America, is most direct on this point. White Americans rarely tell the truth about their racial attitudes. Indeed, Feagin has created an entire theory around racial frames and his research has been so meaningful in unmasking racism that numerous scholars now see an entry into the discourse because Feagin and others have taken the covers off of this very necessary American discussion.

Tim Wise is an acclaimed writer and anti-racist activist. Clearly there has been no more insightful lecturer and author on the race issue than Tim Wise. Over the past thirty years few people have achieved the status of Wise largely because Tim has been able to speak truth to whites in a masterful way. Because he is white I believe that Tim Wise has a peculiar and special insight into the personality and psychology of white Americans. Wise has provided anti-racism training for teachers, physicians and other professional in all 50 states. Perhaps Wise was one of the first people to recognize that the election of Barack Obama demonstrated the durability of racism in a society based on the bedrock of black inferiority and white privilege in every institution. Whites sought to affirm their superiority and their authority with a vengeance not seen in recent memory just as soon as Obama was elected. Wise was one of the few whites brave enough to challenge Right-Wingers gathered to react negatively to Obama.

The legendary Peggy McIntosh had premiered the idea of white privilege as the basis for maintenance of racism. Feagin, Wise, and other activists against racism all pay homage to Peggy McIntosh because she was the first one to itemize the numerous ways whites had privilege in a racist society. In 1989 McIntosh wrote the very famous essay "White Privilege: Unpacking the Invisible Knapsack." It had twenty-one statements about white privilege that circulated around the country as on point as a powerful indictment of racism. One of the statements, number 7, reads, "When I am told about our national heritage or about "civilization," I am shown that people of my color made it what it is." Indeed, the election of President Obama in 2008 as President of the United States of America challenged a plethora of privilege understandings that white racists held.

Obama's campaigns and his elections have not really defied this lesson; they really succeeded because the combined votes of African Americans, Latinos, and Asians were overwhelmingly in support of his candidacy. Senator John McCain beat Obama among white votes by 57% to 43%! That was hardly a case to claim that the American society had become postracial. Actually after the first election the forces of racism in the country redoubled their efforts to insure that Obama not be successful. They were adamant that the election of a black man would create a nation that would become the laughing stock of the world.

Thomas Jefferson had once remarked that he feared that if the enslaved Africans were freed they would have "ten thousand recollections of the crimes committed against them" and would want to take revenge. Deep in the American psyche is this fear of revenge that Jefferson understood to be a normal reaction to the horrors visited upon people. This is why it is considered remarkable, as Anderson Cooper said in response to the killing of Walter Scott in North Charleston, South Carolina in April 2015, that Scott's mother was a deeply religious woman whose faith allowed her to forgive the man who killed her son. This is the regular pattern for many blacks that have witnessed white violence. So the question is, "Why do whites see Barack Obama as a threat?" One could reasonably say that it has a lot to do with the idea of revenge and retaliation even though Obama has followed the same cool and reflective path as Walter Scott's mother.

There is no question in most people's mind in this country that the issue of race is the most dominant aspect of the American society. Almost all casual and a lot of formal, documentary, and legal discourses in the nation include race and racism or racial attitudes. This is not related to one group of people but to the entire country. Not only is race intertwined with the history of the country as I have written in my book, *Erasing Racism: The Survival of the American Nation,* but it is the elephant that many people would like to shove under the carpet rather than to have an honest, open discussion about anti-racism.

Obama's presidency, although deliberately it seemed at first, sought to distance itself from race as much as possible after the Jeremiah Wright incident, was once again brought into the discourse during the last years of his terms. As much as he tried he could not escape the negativity of many white citizens who would push and pull him into as many crevices as they could. In a profoundly courageous expression of dignity and elegance, worthy of the best presidents, he lived above the fray in ways that many of us would not have been able to do. Indeed this was almost necessary given the fact that he was the first African American president in the nation's history. His plate had to be clean; his responses had to be measured; and his rhetoric had to be couched within the framework of history. As a student of Constitutional Law and history he was able to disregard the trivial even when it must have hurt, but he knew also that he was a symbolic figure for millions of Africans around the world. He could not break; he could not demonstrate anger; he had to show patience and wisdom. No other president had to undergo as many attacks on his person as Barack Obama. While some may have disagreed with policies of other presidents, they did not necessary attack them personally or wish their deaths. Obama's tenure as president, consequently, had to teach him that the idealism of his youth was corralled into the enlightened fringes of the nation while the central trunk of the American nation was still racist at its core. I am convinced had Obama responded in kind to the likes of the Italian immigrant Rudy Giuliani or the racist tweets and emails of Ferguson, Missouri police, he would have been reduced to an ordinary man and he wanted most of all for the nation and for African Americans to be seen as good citizens. But why should the President have to entertain the idea of image of African Americans when no white president has ever had to cover for white people in the same way?

What happened to the narrative of Barack Obama's mixed race heritage as a part of his contribution to the American political arena? There is no question that he used it to appeal to a wide segment of the population, but what was the response, the fundamental response of the white population to the mixed race Obama? The fact that he was mixed race was enough for them to see him as a black man and happily he saw himself as a black man since there was no other option in the American society. Since the *Plessy v. Ferguson Decision* in 1896, America, whether legal or not, has accepted in the political mythology the notion that a person with one drop of African blood is an African. It is an old myth that worked for the slave plantation when white men had babies by black women. Were these children white or black? The society by law and practiced defined such children as black and therefore opted for the false notion of the purity of the white race, today; such theories appear infantile but at one time in the American society they were essential to the survival of the system of white supremacy. Homer Plessy's ordeal was a test of the system of racial segregation and separate but equal. He was certainly more white biologically than he was African yet the court ruled against him because he had more than one drop of African blood with the consequence that he could not sit anywhere he wanted in the coach.

Those who detested Obama could not fathom the fact that this man who was born of a white mother and a black father, whom he hardly met, could be president with more than one drop of African blood. Although he had been raised by his white family and spent his childhood mastering his school lessons and his social mores as measured out by conversation and talk in his home, Obama found his longing for freedom, justice, equality, and morality to be so strong that he would later seek to work for the socially downtrodden and the weak and longsuffering in Chicago. Acculturated as an African American by his white mother who obviously knew the America into which he had been born Obama would find his place at the famous and activist Chicago Trinity

Church of Christ with Dr. Jeremiah Wright as his pastor. Trinity remains an outstanding church with a commitment to social justice and Christian character. For about twenty years Obama found his way occasionally to Trinity and he married one of the queens of Chicago's Southside.

Whites who were suspicious of him found his social relations with community workers, black nationalists, Afrocentrists, and Pan Africanists, and revolutionary preachers to be the evidence they sought. He could not represent white interests or white privilege and to the degree that he represented justice as determined by the social conditions of the black community white reactionaries hated him. The website *Obamamustgo* criticized Obama for being married to a woman, Michelle Obama, who said on February 18, 2008, that she was proud of her country for the first time when her husband won an election. Of course, the website sought to spin chaos in the nature of context, history, and social relationships; most people knew that she was expressing a collective cultural response to the profound American response to a progressive African American candidate. Of course, this was not the only comment of the spinners of myth. The website also sought to tar Obama with anti-Semitism and anti-Americanism by claiming that the preacher, Dr. Jeremiah Wright, Jr., had such proclivities; something that could never be proved by any objective observer or researcher. Indeed, Reverend Wright had served the American military as a medic and in his official capacity had assisted in the medical procedure for President Lyndon B. Johnson in 1966. The Trinity Church of Christ in Chicago released a photo showing Reverend Wright standing next to the gurney that held the president. Vice Admiral George Burkley, the president's personal doctor, wrote a letter of commendation to Reverend Wright. This was posted to the church's website.

Later Reverend Wright was one of the prominent religious leaders asked to pray with President Bill Clinton after the Monica Lewinsky affair. The church posted a photo with President Clinton and Reverend Wright in a warm embrace. Wright visited the White House twice during the Clinton Administration. The *ObamaMustGo* campaign sought to smear Obama more with the argument that he was endorsed by Louis Farrakhan and the New Black Panther Party as if the candidate had some how engineered this support. The chaotic thread that was being used to spin anti-Obama rhetoric was based in fear of the unknown.

There was nothing that Obama could do during the First Coming of the President in 2009 that would ease the fears of the anti-Obama forces. If he traveled to Europe, they were frightened that the Europeans would think of the American people as weak because they had elected a black man. If he traveled to Africa, they would claim that he was really not devoted to America but to his father's country. Nevertheless, by 2015 the President was comfortable enough with his history and achievements that he could make a trip to Africa without any concern about what his enemies would say.

A largely symbolic trip to Kenya in July 2015 solidified his identification with Africa and his Kenyan family. I am certain that historians will see the reaction of whites to his triumphant visit to his father's homeland, since Obama himself was born in the United States, as a moment of personal and collective affirmation. For some whites it will confirm what they knew, that he was not an American, and for others it will demonstrate that his interests were not the same as theirs. However, for Obama, it was necessary and historic for him to engage his own personal and presidential history by taking this trip.

The unlikely narrative of Obama's life challenged the American society in profound ways about race. In some places the mixed race narrative may have helped him with liberal whites and blacks but in the South he lost the white vote overwhelmingly because "race-mixing" even while it happens regularly is considered a negative practice to many white southerners. Inheritors of the myth of the purity of the white race and purveyors of white racial domination and superiority could never be at peace with a descendant of Africans in the White House. It was not just accursed but it was an abomination that no amount of prayer or rhetorical flourishes could cleanse from the soul of America. Obama would bring all the "obscenities" that the white racists did not like: federal health care, same sex marriage, race mixing, social liberalism, higher taxes, and possibly other "evils" that they could imagine.

During his first run for the presidency, Obama's lead over

John McCain was sometimes in double digits and polls showed that over 90% of Americans would be comfortable with a black president. This did not translate into 90% voting for Obama on Election Day 2008. The euphoria around the fact that Obama's presence in the race was authentic and dynamic, but it did not last. While the nation was excited that a black man was running, that he was very intelligent, more than qualified for the office, and worldly, with the best American education one could find, paled besides the angst, fear, and anxiety that greeted whites when they awoke to discover that Obama might indeed be the President of the United States. Some even threatened to leave the country and move elsewhere. Such reactions made it clear that winning the presidency would not mean that the problem of racism would be solved or resolved. In fact, the animosity and hatred stirred up by right wing pundits would translate into outright attacks on the President's character.

Rush Limbaugh, perhaps the Dean of Right Wing pundits, bellowed on September 11, 2012, regarding the re-election campaign, "We're doomed." Limbaugh's prophecy was given with the gravitas of foreknowledge, "If Obama is re-elected, it will happen. There is no if about this. And it's gonna be ugly. It's gonna be gut-wrenching, but it will happen. The country's economy is going to collapse if Obama is re-elected. I don't know how long: a year and a half, two years, three years"(retrieved June 28, 2015 from *Newsmax*). Of course, although Russ Limbaugh has the largest fringe pulpit he was not the only one preaching this brand of anti-Obamaism. The musician Ted Nugent, on April 17, 2012 spewed a lot of anti-government vitriol when he said, "We've got four Supreme Court justices who don't believe in the Constitution. Does everybody here know that four of the Supreme Court justices not only determined you don't have the right to keep and bear arms, four Supreme Court Justices signed their name to a declaration that Americans have no fundamental right to self defense? That sounds like a stoned hippie. That doesn't sound like a Supreme Court anything." But he was not through with this line of thinking, this treacherous ideology of claiming that those he disagrees with "do not believe in the Constitution" which is like saying that they are not real Americans; he goes further to say, "If Barack Obama becomes the president in November, again, I will be either be dead or in jail by this time next year." History has shown that the sky did not fall when Obama was elected. In fact, under Obama the economy grew to the point that unemployment that had been 10 percent when he was first elected was only 5 percent by the last year of his presidency. Furthermore, Ted Nugent did not have to leave the country.

One of the great paradoxes about Americans is that individual overt racist acts have become unpopular but racism regardless to how distasteful and vile in the context of public society still exists in collective private actions. Thus, Americans when asked would agree that race should not have been a factor in either of the two

Obama presidential campaigns. However, black Americans will overwhelming confirm that race was a factor in the elections. Whites would sometimes say that their decision to vote against Obama had more to do with his policies than the fact that they have something against his race. My carpenter handyman, a second generation Italian, believes that Obama wants to open the country to let in "all the Mexicans." No matter how much one points out that the United States is largely a nation of immigrants, and that Obama is not trying to destroy the country, you will have some staunch votarists of Russ Limbaugh believing the opposite.

Overt racism may be socially unacceptable in most parts of the nation but covert forms of racism still exist in how people make decisions and order their lives. They could tell you that they support African American candidates and pull the lever in the privacy of the voting booth for white candidates along racial lines. This factor often makes it hard to determine how much stock to put in polls when race plays a part. It is possible that I may be wrong here but it seems to me that blacks have had more experience voting for white candidates than whites have had in voting for blacks. This is precisely why black Americans remain the most progressive ethnic voting bloc in the American electorate. As my father once told me, "Boy, we know this place and we have pushed it forward from the day we got off the ships from Africa." Of course, my father's generation became Democrats during the time of Franklin Delano Roosevelt and the New Deal.

Barack Obama's campaign for the presidency in 2008 came on top of the two earlier campaigns by Shirley Anita St. Hill Chisholm in 1972 and Jesse Jackson in 1984. As they had done during the runs of Chisholm and Jackson many whites used racial epithets to refer to candidate Obama.

To his credit Senator John McCain, the Republican nominee in the 2008 race, had the audacity to challenge some of his supporters whose attitudes about Obama bordered on the irrational. In October 2008, McCain held a town hall meeting that was full of animosity toward Obama and had to tell the audience, "I have to tell you. Senator Obama is a decent person and a person you don't have to be scared of as president of the United States," McCain told a supporter at a town hall meeting in Minnesota who said he was "scared" of an Obama presidency.

"Come on, John!" one white supporter shouted as the crowd, shocked that McCain did not see the threat of Obama as president, hissed in disbelief. They shouted "liar" and "terrorist" in reference to McCain's opponent.

McCain while speaking passed his microphone to a woman who said, "I can't trust Obama. I have read about him and he's not, he's not uh — he's an Arab. He's not ...." McCain retook the microphone and said in a very sincere voice: "No, ma'am. He's a decent family man [and] citizen that I just happen to have disagreements with on fundamental issues and that's what this campaign's all about. He's not [an Arab]."

McCain to his credit did not dignify these types of statements. Certainly being an Arab should not discredit an individual from running for the presidency in any society and definitely not in a multicultural one. The fact that a presidential campaign brought out the most overt forms of racism surprised some but others felt that the nature of racism was based on power relations anyway. Some white people seemed to fear that the election of an African American would mean that at a substantially power level America would lose its power. Of course, there were those during the course of Obama's presidency whose intent was to demonstrate that he could not be a forceful president. Some Republicans seemed to feel that Benjamin Netanyahu, who went to high school in Cheltenham, Pennsylvania, should have been the president of the United States and not Israel. Such was the disdain that some white Americans held for Obama that they would have been willing to abandon the nation than honor their own president. Thus, the racial epithets that were used during the first and the second presidential campaigns were symptomatic of an underlying fear that continued after each Obama victory.

Professor Ama Mazama, senior fellow at the Molefi Kete Asante Institute for Afrocentric Studies says, "Racism has not disappeared but what has dissipated is the structural supports for overt racist behaviors even though those institutions are themselves parts of the problem of covert racism" (Ama Mazama, "Frances Cress Welsing and the Cress Theory of Color Confrontation," *Afrocentricity*

International, November 19, 2015) Other researchers have concluded as David Bositis, a senior researcher at the Joint Center for Political and Economic Studies in Washington, did about white racists "They can rant and rave all they want, but time has passed them by." (*Christian Science Monitor,* October 22, 2008).

Nevertheless it was thought by some blacks that Obama's chances at being elected in 2008 would be undermined by latent racism. Fortunately the demographics of the election created a unique opportunity for Barack Obama to win the first election. African Americans whose complexion often allows them to pass for white or white Americans who have identified with blacks such as Rachel Donezal, a white woman who passed for black until 2015, hear racist comments regularly from their white acquaintances. Indeed Sonia Whittle, a Mexican-American, married to a white Republican man, said she often picked up "the scuttlebutt on the streets of Forest Park, a largely black and Hispanic neighborhood in Georgia." Because of her appearance, some people think she only speaks Spanish, but she overhears lots of racial talk every day. She says, "race overshadows all other issues at the moment."

Ms. Whittle did not think the country was ready for an African-American president in 2008 yet Obama won the election and there was no chaos. The country did not fall apart; the sky did not collapse, and if anything happened, it was the determined efforts of a young elected president to regain the economic stability of a failed economy.

Obviously electing an African American as President was a giant step for Americans. Former Mississippi Governor William Winter had once said that he thought Obama's election would be great for racial reconciliation. Of course, Winter was perhaps too much of an optimist when it came to racial reconciliation but what the election in 2008 did suggest was that electing a black man did not mean that the country would be destroyed. Winter may have been right about the image of the United States as the leader of the free world however when he predicted the world would look at the nation differently I believe that Winter did have a point. Americans, on the other hand, not the world in general but some Americans in particular, held strong opinions against the president. After Obama had been in office for the first four years a poll taken in October 2012, found that racial attitudes had really gotten worst since the country elected its first black president. Depictions of the president as a chimpanzee, gorilla, monkey or lion, and as a caricature of a human being seemed to go hand-in-hand with bumper stickers on cars calling for impeachment of the President and insulting other black Americans. Many African Americans I talked with felt that the reaction of whites to the election of Obama was to demonstrate that they were still in charge; it was an overreaction that led to the increased incidents of racial hostility. The Associated Press reported that a slight majority of whites expressed prejudice against African Americans, probably the same majority of whites who voted against Obama and for the McCain-Palin ticket. According to the survey 51% of Americans expressed explicit anti-black attitudes in 2012 as compared with 48% in a similar 2008 survey. The Associated Press says, "When measured by an implicit racial attitudes test, the number of Americans with anti-black sentiments jumped to 56%, up from 49% during the last presidential election. In both tests, the share of Americans expressing pro-black attitudes fell." Consequently there was no decline in prejudice because a black man had been elected to the White House; on the contrary the attitudes against blacks hardened and might be considered the results of a feeling of powerless ness on the parts of many whites. One of the developers of the survey, Jon Krosnick of Stanford University said, "As much as we'd hope the impact of race would decline over time ... it appears the impact of anti-black sentiment on voting is about the same as it was four years ago." Nothing in the campaign prepared those who believed in the Obama dream for the reaction of the extreme right. The cycle of America has been the push and the pull of social change. "We have this false idea that there is uniformity in progress and that things change in one big step. That is not the way history has worked," said Jelani Cobb, professor of history and director of the Institute for African-American Studies at the University of Connecticut, "When we've seen progress, we've also seen backlash."

Although Jelani Cobb does not explain the reasons for this racial backlash at the presumption of progress it is probably the direct result of a psychological adjustment to the continuing growth of black and white consciousness about race. There can be no meaningful discussion in the country about race until it is admitted that racism exists. While Obama spent much of his first term in office trying to avoid talking about race, somehow buying into the "mythe du vide" his second term has been overtaken by racial animosity although never identified as such by the Republican right wing. The Republicans saw their assaults as necessary to prevent the president from succeeding. Mitch McConnell went so far as to say that his idea was to insure that Obama would not be successful. I am not able to recall either in experience or in history when an American politician had expressed that he wanted to see his president fail. What animus could drive this type of behavior on the part of a nation's representatives or senators? How could a nation legitimately accept such politicians as serving the interests of the nation when in fact they are serving a small minority of bigots?

Yet the Second Coming of Obama in 2012 was indicative of bizarre election politics. In West Virginia, the electorate gave 41 percent of their vote to a white convicted fellow rather than to the incumbent president. How could a white convict beat an incumbent president who had done an incredibly good job at the presidency despite the opposition? Who could explain the dislike of the president in rational terms? Of course, it is easy to say that Obama had championed climate change policies, negotiating with Iran, realignment with Cuba, modernizing the national infrastructure and electric grid, supporting the automobile industry, ending the Iraq war, closing the Afghanistan war, bringing gas prices down, growing the economy as reflected in the stock market, initiating immigration reforms, re-organizing the financial institutions, and seeking to tax the one percent of the nation's super rich. Obama's administration saw a growth of the economy of over 5 percent by December 2014 and that was more than it had been in ten years. Furthermore, his keystone legislation of Affordable Health Care Act did not bring double-digit inflation as it had been predicted. After the passage of the law the economy actually got better and so did the employment figures just as Obama's Administration had predicted.

The racial animosity asserted itself in a political sense when it was reported that in the history of the American nation half of the 168 filibusters against a presidential nomination to the judiciary or White House office had been launched during President Barack Obama's first five years in office! Clearly there was bitterness against President Obama that went far beyond the disagreements opposition members had with other presidents. Even during the days of Civil Rights debates and arguments the viciousness against presidents who were committed to equality did not approach the vile and abusive nature of the attacks on President Obama. John Kennedy, Lyndon Johnson, Jimmy Carter, Bill Clinton had their detractors but the Republicans came after the first black president with a viciousness that had no precedent in history.

Obama is a historical figure whose election as President of the United States has come to signify many paradoxes. He was a first term Senator who ran for the highest office in the land and won. He was an only son raised by a single white mother and an Indonesian step-father, and then by his white grandparents; he was also married to a black woman with an aura that was significant in her own right and had two beautiful daughters. He would become the first black man elected in an overwhelmingly white country. But in saying all of these incredibly interesting facts one cannot forget that Obama was not elected with a white majority. The majority of whites who voted in both elections that he won for the presidency voted for his opponents. The crux of his presidency, actually the cross that he has had to bear, is the dislike that many whites held for him. Of course, some Democratic contributors also took the opportunity to express racial anxieties like when Amy Pascal, president of SONY Entertainment, commented in emails that President Obama enjoyed movies such as *Django, 12 Years a Slave,* or *Butler*. Some ultra-rightists felt from the beginning that Obama was out to take "their country" away from them. If he did not give it to the communists, he surely would give it to the Africans or the Muslims. The conservative Republican wit Dinesh D'Souza claimed that President Obama had some special problem with being an American because of the colonial status of his father's country under Britain at one time. Indeed, the United States was once a British colony. These facts never mean anything to irrational arguments that are based on race and as we have seen often enough you do not have to be a white man to make racist comments and arguments. What D'Souza expressed were the thoughts and fears expressed in the many negative things white racists had said about the President of the United States of America. Long an anti-black pundit D'Souza, an Indian from Goa, and Bobby Jindal, the Indian governor of Louisiana, seemed to take special pleasure in attacking the first African American president.

The monumentality of Barack Obama's election to the White House is not merely in his being the first person of clear African descent to be so elected, but the severe moment of America's triumph was a victory of the future over the past. I have written it this way because there has long been discussion about the possibility that Thomas Jefferson, Andrew Jackson, Abraham Lincoln, Warren Harding, and Calvin Coolidge had African ancestry. Joel A. Rogers and Auset Bahkhufu have written books demonstrating the possible evidence, based on the one-drop rule, that at least five American presidents before Barack Obama had African ancestry. Indeed, one of the best cases is that of Warren G. Harding, the 29th president who served from 1921 until 1923. It is said that Harding never denied his African ancestry. When some politicians asked him to deny his African ancestry, Harding is said to have replied, "How should I know whether or not one of my ancestors might have jumped the fence?" William Chancellor, a Wooster College professor of politics wrote a book on the Harding family genealogy which identified African ancestors in the families of both of his parents. It is alleged that Justice Department agents bought and destroyed all copies of this book. Chancellor had also written that Harding attended Central College in Iberia College that was set up to help educate fugitives from slavery.

CHAPTER TWO

The Rise of Racial Hostility

The United States rose in the 19th and 20th centuries as a world power with its own vision about its place in history. That vision was shaped, molded, and cast by numerous presidents and politicians who argued for a democratic future that would be a beacon for the rest of the world. It is true that after the nation was born in infamy with enslavement of Africans and the dispossession of the Native Peoples it worked for the first 218 years to correct the problems included in the founding documents. The enslavement of Africans had begun before the birth of the nation and the first 76 years under the Constitution were years of diabolical practices, horrible conditions for health and life of Africans, and the use of the Holy Bible and its interpreters as defenders of a system that could not be defended rationally. There would not have been, could not have been, an Obama during those years. And because there was never a true Revolution that overturned the system of white privilege from 1865 to 1968 the nation struggled to right the most obvious wrongs through protests and legislation. So, Obama's election in 2008 changed the nature of the country's politics and pointed toward a more positive future.

Obama did not come to the presidency devoid of talent, skill, credentials, and intellect. He mastered the techniques of his profession, preparing himself in the trenches of American education, working in the Inner Cities, studying Constitutional Law, and serving the poor. In some ways, he was one of the most qualified candidates ever to run for public office. Thus, the first presidential election of Barack Obama cannot be dismissed as a fluke; it cannot be gainsaid. It must be recognized as a pivotal point in race relations, the perceptions of Africans and the image of the United States. No one can ignore these achievements. I am not so enamored that I cannot see that it comes fraught with some of the most disturbing collateral issues that we have confronted in this era. To some degree, it was assumed by many African Americans that the attacks on black males by police and vigilante groups during the Obama presidency were directly caused by the fact that a black man occupied the White House. It is easy to make this assumption when one does not see the long history of racial brutality and injustice. Laying the blame on Obama's election may happen because his election concentrated the thinking of the press, the community, and the police on examples of racial profiling.

I am sure that in some circles there were people who believed that the election of Barack Obama would mean that America had crossed the threshold of race. Elements of the society spoke passionately about the end of racism, the post racial generation emerged as a free, respectful, and liberated people, all the time while those with more sinister, hardline, and diabolical attitudes gathered their anger and shaped their rhetoric toward the man who would become and who became president. What the verbal, symbolic, and media attacks on Obama showed was the peculiar pettiness of racism and the elegant, almost pitying, attitude of Obama who never once replied in kind to the racist attacks on him. As we shall see in this book he attempted to credit his attackers with high motives until the last years of his presidency when he became somewhat more combative but even then less Doberman than his friends would have had him exhibit. Obama struggled, I believe, internally with how best to approach the white population that soured on his election almost as soon as he took the office. Afterall, his mother was white and that had been a part of his narrative. Yet it was the whites that most wished to choke hold him to the ground although he had scores of black detractors as well. However, blacks who criticized him, as in my case, built cases on the grounds of progressive politics. We wanted to see a more robust policy toward African nations, a more domestic-oriented gaze toward the poor and homeless, and an Obama legacy toward justice that would correct the sins of the enslavement, and so forth. None of this was based on Obama's race, color, origins, or creed. Blacks who wrote critiques only did so to encourage the president to move more aggressively against racism and poverty.

On the other hand, while there were whites that had principled objections to some of Obama's policies most of the whites that attacked him were vicious enough to insult the president and to attempt to neuter him while he was in office. To his credit he became a skilled fighter who fought against his enemies with coolness and organization.

Michael Tillotson, the University of Pittsburgh professor, has characterized much of the animosity toward black people as an agency reduction formation. Whenever there is an attempt to advance toward some form of autonomy of action there is always a white reaction. This reaction has been demonstrated in police brutality cases as well as political blockages. Quite interestingly, Tillotson's analysis of the internal security of African Americans was published during the tenure of President Obama. I would not say that this book could not have been written at some other point but it is clear to me that the campaign and election of Obama had a lot to do with the concentration of our minds on reaction to blackness, that is, reaction to African people's advance in any capacity. I heard college professors declare that the racism on their campuses, the assaults on those who sought tenure, the resistance to administrative appointments of black people to high level posts, and the severe challenges faced in classes by black students were all the results of Obama's victories. I know no empirical proof of any of this but it was the expressed feeling of many African Americans who interpreted their troubles to white reaction to Obama. Of course, the episodes of hostility to the president do make the case that Obama was a lightning rod to many whites, and some other people, namely Dinesh D'Souza and Bobby Jindal, two Indian-Americans who heaped quite a bit of vitriol on Obama as well. There were others as well who sniped from the margins and created fake firestorms of resentment where none was needed.

The Obama era, which I date from his announcement on February 10, 2007 in Springfield, Illinois, for the Presidency, has been characterized by three prominent national characteristics: *a rhetoric of post-raciality, new hostilities against blacks*, and the *attempt to diminish the presidency*. These are the traits of a political lynching and in a way they are reminiscent of what happened during the 20th century when physical lynching was quite common. I recall reading a newspaper piece from July 2, 1903 issue of the *Chicago Record –Herald* about a mob of fifty white men who shot and killed Ruben Elrod at his house in Columbia, South Carolina. Three women who lived in the house were warned to leave the county after being stripped and flogged by the men the report says, "No reason was given for the attack."

There was another account of lynching that appeared in the *Montgomery Advertiser* on August 1, 1910. The paper reported "fifteen to twenty negroes were hunted down and killed by a mob of 200 or 300 men near Palestine, Texas without any real cause at all, according to Sheriff Black."

What strikes me is the fact that the reporters tend to say that there did not seem to be any reason for the lynching. If you asked many of the whites who were hostile to Obama's presidency why were they so disrespectful, they would probably demur and say that they 'did not have a reason." It is almost as if they believe that fighting Obama was a natural thing to do. Despite the concurrent arguments about postraciality brought on by Obama's election the negative side was equally as strong as the positive side of his national election.

The contemporary writer Touré has written a book called *Who's Afraid of Post-Blackness,* a book with a truly unfortunate title. I do not think anyone has ever made a big fuss about post-blackness. What people are scared of, including some blacks, is blackness itself. Touré claims that he used to read works by Asante and Maulana Karenga when he was a teenager; I sincerely and seriously wish that he had continued to read our writings because I believe he would have seen that there was never and will not be in the near future in the United States either post-blackness or postracialism. He would have discovered that the fear in America is neither post-blackness nor postraciality; it remains the fear of race itself, however it is constructed along lines of white privilege. Anything that threatens white privilege based on color will find challenges among white people. One can imagine what mortal fear wrapped its arms around white racists when they knew that a black man would become President of the United States of America.

From the time of the first US census, 1790, to the late 1800s, the US recognized four races: white, black, American Indian, and mulatto. Eventually Chinese was added as a racial group in the late 19th century. Mulatto disappeared from the census around 1910 partly due to the fact that possibly thirty percent or more of the African American population had white patriarchy due to white plantation owners raping black women during the 17th and 18th centuries. By 1900 the mulatto population was so intertwined with the purely African population that it was impossible to tell who was mulatto and who was not; in fact, the mulatto was classified as black. In the census of 1930 the category "Mexican" appeared but was never repeated. However, by 1980 Hispanic appears for the first time in the census. In this instance the idea of Hispanic origin was anyone with a heritage, nationality, lineage, or parents or ancestors from a Spanish-speaking. People who identify as Hispanic, Latino, or Spanish may be any race.

On the other hand, the idea of race and people of African descent is problematized by the infamous "one-drop" rule. The legal thinking that came out of the *Plessy v. Ferguson* decision in the late 19th century unquestionably spearheaded this movement to classify all people with 'one drop" of African blood as African. This irrational decision has plagued racial discourse in America. Plessy was a light-skinned individual who lived in the black community of New Orleans, conducted himself as a part of the black community's culture, and was known to be affiliated and associated with black skinned people. However, when he got on the train he sat in the "whites only" section. This precipitated a legal action that went to the Supreme Court. Although Plessy was more white than black genetically, the Court decided that any person with "one drop" of African blood was an African, hence the "one drop" rule for racial classification.

Had Plessy been able to make his case then the United States system of racial classification would be closer to that of Brazil where people can make decisions of race on the basis of origin, color, or culture. Nevertheless, the census of the United States has been a political document in terms of classifying populations. For example, Hispanicity came into permanence in 1970 as an example of the changing racial characteristics of the society and by 1980 was on the US Census. Prior to Hispanics, people from Mexico or Cuba could be seen as Black or White people who spoke Spanish. This could become quite complicated when it was recognized that you can have people of African origin in Cuba, Mexico, or Colombia, who speak Spanish. Hispanic, therefore, became a cultural term in the census but often did not satisfy those people who were born, for example, in Costa Rica but who claimed an African heritage. People born in Brazil do not claim to be Hispanic because the language of that large South American country is Portuguese.

President Barack Obama's campaign and elections thrust into the American discourse on race an intense debate over post-raciality. William Julius Wilson, a Harvard professor had written a book while at the University of Chicago, *The Declining Significance of Race,* in which he claimed that the life chances of black people had more to do with economic opportunities than with race. He was roundly criticized by liberals, black and white, and sent back to the library and computer lab for further work and reflection on this argument.

Clearly race had not gone anywhere in the discourse about injustice and inequality; it was as real as it had ever been. Yet what Wilson projected was a vision where race would not be a major aspect of our discussions about poverty and life chances. With the campaign of Barack Obama and his clarion declaration that "there was not a Blue State or Red State America, there is not a white America or a black America, there is just the United States of America" we had leaped into the Wilsonian discourse about post-raciality. But Obama had dreamed of a new America when he announced his run for the White House. He had sought to bring progressive forces together to bridge important chasms. This is what he said in the Springfield address:

"That's why I'm in this race.

Not just to hold an office, but to gather with you to transform a nation.

I want to win that next battle — for justice and opportunity.

I want to win that next battle — for better schools, and better jobs, and health care for all.

I want us to take up the unfinished business of perfecting our union, and building a better America.

And if you will join me in this improbable quest, if you feel destiny calling, and see as I see, a future of endless possibility stretching before us; if you sense, as I sense, that the time is now to shake off our slumber, and slough off our fear, and make good on the debt we owe past and future generations, then I'm ready to take up the cause, and march with you, and work with you. Together, starting today, let us finish the work that needs to be done, and usher in a new birth of freedom on this Earth."

Obama did not venture to obliterate race, but he did throw his hat into the ring of those who argued that unity of the American nation was more important than race. This instant spurred the post racial moment and gave birth to many articles and commentaries on the new reality. At any rate, the statistics regarding interracial marriages showed a steady increase in the number of such unions since 1980. Elevating the ideas of skill and merit to the forefront of contemporary narratives about social structures authors and media pundits welcomed the coming of the post-racial age.

The emergence of the Tea Party Republicans at the precise

moment of Obama's presidential ambitions was seen as an epoch changing direction for the country but the real problem with the Right Wing of the Republican Party was the fact that the world in its explosive technological, social, and cultural dynamism had left them behind. They were and are still fighting the battles of the early 1960s and they have no understanding of Kinshasa with 13 million people, or Nairobi with 10 million people, or Lagos with 28 million people. They still think New York is the biggest city in the world because they are buried in the narrow politics of race. They do not know that the United States does not have the fastest train in the world; that distinction belongs to China. They do not understand that Zimbabwe is one of the top literate countries in the world. I remember being quite happy when Sarah Palin made her first trip out of the country; just perhaps she would be sobered by knowing a little bit more about the world. Alas, some can see and still not know. Like many of her Tea Party compatriots, Sarah Palin misjudged the character of the American people. Since the turn of this century the United States has become more liberal in its outlook on social, moral, legal, and intellectual ideas. Old attitudes mired in the mud of a fearful era will not carry the future; only those who are bold enough to asset a new direction will win the day.

Many blacks believe that the election of Barack Obama unleashed new forms of racism. Black bloggers characterized the reaction to Obama's election as a *blacklash* just like the *backlash* after the passage of Civil Rights legislation decades ago.

Reactionary talk radio harps on the anti-Obama theme 24 hours a day. In one twenty four hour period Fox News mentioned Obama's name negatively 568 times.

Conservative talk show hosts show no respect for the Office of the President, seeking every opportunity to ridicule him. If he is a Harvard trained lawyer; he is too smart; if he were a community organizer, he worked for Saul Alinsky, a sneaky way to identify him with the Jewish left; if he has an international outlook that see America as one of the major players; he is too soft on foreign policy. If he believes in diplomacy rather than gunboat force, he is giving in to America's enemies. If he chastises Israel for bombing the hell out of Gaza in an unequal war, then he is considered an enemy of Israel. Of course, none of this sticks to him because these caricatures have little basis in political reality. Obama got the United States out of Iraq, he eliminated the threat from Osama bin Laden, he gave the country for the first time national health care, and he demonstrated that he could compete with anyone when it came to international politics. Hostility aside, Obama intensified his political ambitions during his second term, preparing and opening political relationships with Cuba, creating new arenas for gay Americans, and seeking to re-commit to financial investment in Africa, among many other activities.

Lynching involves the idea of diminishing the person. In the case of Obama those who sought to destroy him went after the Office of the Presidency itself. It would not be easy for Obama to make headway on many of the promises he made during his campaign because the Tea Party legislators and their allies would block any progressive legislation. They would work to demonstrate that the "black President" could not and would not be successful.

Knowledge creates more ignorance in the sense that the more one knows about something the greater the ignorance of what there is to know. It is like opening the door a little to see what is in the room; only when the door is wide open can you see the entire picture. The Presidency, according to the Constitution, is an important office. Indeed, the only officers of state elected nationally are the president and the vice president; no senator or representative or member of the Supreme Court, holds that distinction.

The American president, however, is neither an emperor nor a king, and the power of the presidency is derived from the masses of the people. This said, it is the most powerful post that can be held by a mortal on earth. No king or emperor wields more raw military power, financial wealth, persuasive appeal than the American president. The President of the United States can plunge the world into an annihilating war with the push of a button; the President can suggest an idea and others will carry it out in a timely fashion; and the President can unify the nation like no other public figure can do. It is an awesome power.

The person who gains the Presidency has outsmarted and outcampaigned some of the most intelligent and ambitious people on earth. To do it once is an extraordinary achievement, but to do it twice is magnificent. Those who have held the office twice, for eight years, are in a special class of presidents. President Barack Obama, a black man, became the most powerful human on the earth when he was first elected in 2008!

During the two terms of his administration his own countrymen, including the Congress, have challenged Obama with more bitterness than he received from most enemies abroad. Under the Republican leadership the Congress of the United States blocked almost all of his major initiatives during his first term. Had it not been for the brief period when he had a Democratic majority during his first two years many of the achievements that strengthened the nation would not have been made. Achieving infrastructural change would have made a great difference in the employment situation in the nation had the President been able to find partners among the Republicans. Nevertheless the economy improved and the unemployment figures went down during his second term. The Bureau of Labor Statistics declared in November 2015 that the unemployment rate was at 5.0 percent. One has to recall that Obama really saved the economy after its collapse in 2008 and went on to bail out the automobile industry. He could have done even more with willing and cooperative partners in Congress. However, if your enemies would rather see the country lose than to support the your policies then as President you are in a serious battle. There has been no time that Obama was not in battle with the legislators. People who do not believe that the climate is changing because of humans will not believe that a black man could be president.

Scholars and philosophers considered the reason for the disdain of this president? The Presidency, while not a kingship, is a very distinguished post but beyond the ordinary aspect of the job of the president, the Office of the Presidency, apart from any particular person is central to the American Democracy. The President is also the Head of State since the United States does not have a king or a queen. Just as Americans have been taught through school and example to respect the Constitution, the flag, and the Declaration of Independence, they have also been encouraged to respect the Office of the Presidency. One may not like the person who occupies the office for many reasons, but because the person who occupies the office holds the majority of the American people's confidence the office is symbolic of the nation. Nevertheless, disrespect for the office during the time of Barack Obama has been unabated among Right Wing Republicans.

It is impossible to think of an era when the President of the United States of America was considered someone who did not love the country. In fact, the enemies of Obama claim that the President of Israel, Benjamin Netanyahu, had more to say about the security of the United States and Israel than the President of the United States. Speaker John Boehner's invitation on January 21, 2015 to Netanyahu to address a joint session of the American Congress on the Iran Deal without any consultation with the

President was a deliberate undermining of the executive in line with the diminution of the office.

Thus, when Netanyahu arrived in Washington on March 1, 2015 he came with an idea to push the Congress to force the President to change negotiating policies with Iran. It was not so much the calculation of Netanyahu that was on display, although it was, but it was really the fact that Speaker John Boehner's relationship with a black president had soured even more than it had during the first term and that he was determined to stoke the political fires against the President that caused some to say that Boehner's actions should have brought charges of treason. Thus, the Republican leader and the Israelis President found symmetry in their resistance to the liberalism touted by a president who believed that it was essentially immoral for Israel to be comfortable with the fact that millions of people who live in Israel do not have citizenship or have second class citizenship, but that the President of the United States should not negotiate with an enemy of the country. Obama's liberalism was at odds with Boehner's conservative Republicanism and Netanyahu's conservative Likud politics. As Obama was fond of saying, "You don't negotiate with your friends; you negotiate with your enemies."

One might also say that Boehner unfortunately missed an opportunity to be a transformative Speaker of the House because of his own lack of hubris and a Republican caucus that was so far right that he could not see the historical reality staring him in the face. When he announced his resignation after he had invited Pope Francis to speak to the United States Congress in September 2015 one saw a broken man, sad as a historical figure, seeking to recover a bit of the glory that could have been his as a working partner with a president who was sure to be seen as transformative. The fact that Boehner could not even accept this role, when the president was not a revolutionary and certainly left many issues on the table that could have been dealt with from the bully pulpit, shows that he held a dim view of the future of the nation. One only has to examine how Obama handled issues with Boehner as well as with his political enemies.

Obama's sense of history was in full form when he tried to solve the political disconnect with Iran over the nuclear issue. Obama sought to have a rapprochement with Iran, one of the longstanding enemies of the United States since the days of the overthrow of the Shah of Iran, and this was not to the liking of some Republicans.

Yet what Boehner did by inviting Benjamin Netanyahu to the Congress was of a different ilk. He sought to embarrass the president by hosting a man who was not the leader of the United States but who was seeking to directly influence the American government.

The Israeli President in an almost unprecedented manner stepped his foot into the political waters of America with the intent of preventing the American president from making a treaty with another government. President Obama's aim to normalize relations with Iran so long as Iran gave up any ambition to build a nuclear bomb was a clear-sighted vision about the relationship between nations. America does not and cannot control the world and it definitely does not have the right nor the duty or will to push Iran around simply because Israel prefers to have Iran sanctioned. Obama correctly perceived, with the backing of major nations in the world, that the historic nation of Persia, Iran, could not continue to be isolated from the world. Furthermore, the more than one hundred billion dollars of Iranian money held in international banks because of sanctions on the country was not under American authority. Yet many pundits and even Republican presidential candidates rushed to tell Americans that "Obama is giving the Iranians 100 billion dollars," although most of them, I suspect, knew that this was Iranian money from the start and that if some nation had embargoed American money for whatever reason we would have had politicians as shrill as those in Iran calling for war with whoever wanted to prevent us from using our own money regardless of the reasons for the embargo. Fortunately for the United States the Harvard and Columbia trained American president was a student of history, law, and politics, and did not believe in government by boast or bombast. He set his mind to a project and he sought to accomplish it.

Nevertheless the Republican attempt to diminish the presidency by attacking Obama on every issue and at every instance where they thought they had an opening proved to be useless because during his second term Obama operated as if he had no political fear. He certainly did not rush to make deals with those who had bedeviled his first term. His interest, it seemed, was to create actions and processes that depended solely on what he could do without the Congress. Freed from the need to be elected he literally seemed to enjoy the office, needling where he needed to, the Republican house and Senate majorities, for their lack of action. When House Speaker John Boehner resigned in the Fall of 2015 he had already fallen from grace with the President. He had sought to lead a tough opposition but without the gravitas necessary to bend his majority toward the will of the masses. Boehner was a captive of a small clique of Right Wing politicians whose ambition was to destroy the first black president. Obama retained his cool, allowed his enemies to attack while needling them here and there, with the kind of intelligence that we had come to expect from the law professor.

Clearly, the iconic racial history of the Obama Era will not be the celebratory embracing of difference and diversity or the kindly sensitivity that comes with context and understanding, but rather it will be the increased visibility of the police murders of young black men. In one year, between the uprisings in Ferguson, Missouri, over the death of Michael Brown, more than 700 young black males were slaughtered in the urban streets of America. Obama's presidency began with the killing of Trayvon Martin in Sanford, Florida, by George Zimmerman. It would be marked by more names of young black males added to the death list. In one year, 2014, police killed these unarmed black people and others. Dontre Hamilton of Milwaukee, Eric Garner of New York, John Crawford of Dayton, Ezell Ford of Florence, California, Dante Parker of Victorville, California, Tanisha Anderson of Cleveland, Akai Gurley of Brooklyn, Tamir Rice of Cleveland, Rumain Brisbon of Phoenix, Jerame Reid of Bridgeton, New Jersey, Tony Robinson of Madison, Wisconsin, Phillip White of Vineland, New Jersey, Eric Harris of Tulsa, Walter Scott of North Charleston, South Carolina, and Freddie Gray of Baltimore, are names of individuals who may very well be called lynching victims of the Obama Era. Anger at Obama rushed to the streets and the neighborhoods from the high chambers of Congress. What the politicians said reverberated to the streets and there were those who believed that Obama was giving the country to blacks, Asians and Latinos. They felt that whites were losing power and were not able to change the reality. So they made Obama the "minority president" regardless of his talk about "no Red States and no Blue States, only the United States of America." These loyalists of the white right saw only a black president.

Those who called him the "Food Stamp President" with no concrete reason failed in the face of the pace of job creation after the 2008 Depression that Obama had inherited. There was only ill-will in the designation; certainly no objective evidence was every presented to prove the accusation.

I think it is important to place the Obama Presidency in a historical perspective and examine the role the presidency can and cannot play in the emergence of a national identity. Nearly one hundred and seventy five years ago there was a period when the elements that constitute tremendous change and the verge of transformation were also present in the nation. It was the 1850s in the United States.

The Fugitive Slave Act formed a central part of the "Compromise of 1850." The white Americans who were against slavery fought to have the state of California admitted into the Union as a free state. They also argued that slave trading should be prohibited in the Federal District of Columbia. However, the slaveholders said that they would agree to those provisions only if the other abolitionists would agree to concessions with regard to slaveholding in Texas and the passage of the Fugitive Slave Law.

What was this law? It provided that escaped Africans be brought back to their slaveholders from anywhere in the nation. If an African escaped from Alabama and went to Michigan she could be apprehended by anyone and taken into custody and returned to the slaveholder. If the person was free and was apprehended on the streets of Ypsilanti she could be taken into bondage on the word of the person who had captured her. All the apprehender had to do was to pay ten dollars, in some cases, five dollars to a magistrate and take the person into custody. Needless to say, no black person was free of this threat.

Passage of this law was so hated by Africans and abolitionists, however, that its existence played a role in the end of slavery a little more than a dozen years later. This law also sparked a more serious movement to Canada since nowhere in the United States was safe. Well-known blacks left the United States and traveled to Ontario, many of their descendants remain there to this day. Driven by fear that their freedom, land, houses, wives and children would be taken into slavery many prominent black agitators purchased guns to defend their families.

This was the Second Fugitive Slave Act. There had been one in 1793. Northern whites had routinely violated the law's provisions and few blacks considered it serious. Now the Southerners demanded that there be tighter controls on fugitives if the North actually wanted these free states in the West. Thus, the law of 1850 tried to close the gaps by demanding that the states' officers and magistrates could be fined up to 1000 dollars if they did not support the slave-hunters in turning in escaped Africans. Furthermore, the act made it possible for slave-catchers to get permission from magistrates to transport Africans back across states' lines without written documentation. No African could make a case in court against the word of a white man. Many free blacks were therefore snatched from the streets of northern cities and taken into slavery. The law forced whites to support the arrests or be liable for the one thousand dollar fine. Hard thinking whites finally understood that the law was unenforceable and in the end fugitives traveled around the states and into Canada.

This entire context had been drawn up by several actions on behalf of the enslaved population. The rise of the Underground Railroad, a series of safe houses that helped Africans escape to the North, the agitation of the abolitionists, especially Charles Remond and Frederick Douglas, supporting by William Lloyd Garrison, and other white abolitionists, and the increased desperation of the Southern planters for forced labor led to a political stalemate between the North and the South. By 1840 the war of Cass County, Michigan had brought the issue to the forefront with Michigan taking center stage. There was a growing African population in Cass County in the 1840s as more and more blacks found a haven close to the Canadian border. Quakers who disliked discriminatory laws, low-priced lands, and liberty kept attracting Africans to Michigan. Southern slaveholders in Boone and Bourbon counties in Kentucky heard about Cass County and sent armed slave catchers to the area to recapture runaways in 1847 and then again in 1849. They failed each time. This infuriated the southern planters who could not stand to see the Michigan blacks living independent lives with their freedom intact. Therefore, they demanded the Fugitive Slave Act of 1850.

On September 18, 1850 the Congress of the United States passed the law and President Millard Fillmore signed it.

It was denounced and nullified by several northern states who refused to obey it, including Vermont and Wisconsin. In fact, a few white ministers continued to help Africans leave the United States for Canada in defiance of the law. Reverend Luther Lee, preacher for the Wesleyan Methodist Church of Syracuse, New York wrote in 1855:

> "I never would obey it. I had assisted thirty slaves to escape to Canada during the last month. If the authorities wanted anything of me, my residence is at 39 Onondaga Street, I would admit that and they could take me and lock me up in the Penitentiary on the hill; but if they did such a foolish thing as that I had friends enough on Onondaga County to level it to the ground before the next morning."

By 1853, the first Black Nationalist thinker, Martin Delany of Pittsburgh had found his voice against the Fugitive Slave Law: "Honorable Mayor: whatever ideas of liberty, I may have, I have learned from reading the lives of your revolutionary fathers. I have therein learned from those ideas that a man has a right to defend his castle with his life, even to the taking of life. Sir my house is my castle. In that castle are none but my wife and my children as free as the angels of heaven, and with a liberty as sacred as the pillars of God. If any man shall approach that house in search of a slave, I care not who he may be, constable, sheriff, magistrate, or judge of the supreme court, no, let it be he who signed this act into law, Millard Fillmore, himself, with his cabinet as his bodyguard, the declaration of independence wavering above his head as his banner, the constitution of his country on his breast as his shield, if he crosses the threshold of my door, and enters my house, and I do not lay him a lifeless corpse at my feet, I hope the grave may refuse my body a resting place and righteous heaven my spirit a home. O, No, he cannot enter my house and we both live."

Obama's elections took place during a time when the American nation no longer held complete sway over the political affairs of the world as it had done for a few years after the fall of the Soviet Union. The United States remained a superpower but it was a power shared increasingly by the energized Chinese economy and the various other regional states that had found their own voices through industry and good fortune such as India, Brazil, South Africa, and Korea. Japan, Germany, France, and Britain still controlled considerable economic and political influence in the world. By the time of Obama's election the George W. Bush legacy had diminished the role of the United States in foreign power, economic, moral influence, and economic leadership. The earlier Ronald Reagan's strut had been reduced and the armies of America were bogged down fighting wars in Iraq and Afghanistan that were remnants of the response to the September 11, 2001 attacks on the nation. Obama would unleash the forces that would kill Osama bin Laden, the mastermind of al-Qaeda yet find himself unable to disentangle America forces from Southwest Asian conflicts.

China was emerging as the second largest economy in the world and the Chinese and American economies were increasingly interlocked in trade relations. Russia under the Putin and Medvedev game of chairs was gaining its feet and able to exercise hegemony in the vicinity of its borders. The Arab Spring blossomed and died all during the Obama Administration. Deals were made and deals had to be made for the United States to nuance the control it could muster under the changing military and political conditions. One can look to the desperation with which the United States has grown aware of the African continent as the new battleground for resources. To be correct, however, it was George W. Bush and his Secretaries of State, Colin Powell and Condolezza Rice who jump started a much more active African strategy than President Bill Clinton.

When George W. Bush left office it is possible that U.S. military assistance agreements were already in place with 53 African countries. The United States is "the principal military partner of most African countries," according to *Afrol News* (September 23, 2015).

While Obama's policies created strains and stresses within the progressive and black communities, nothing approaching the vile and obscene language of the Tea Partyers ever erupted from the mouths of the most visible progressive critics. Even Tavis Smiley and Cornel West could not be said to attack the president because of his race or color. But like many other critics who were disturbed by both domestic and foreign policies I believed that the president had poor advice on African questions. This is not to say that they were not bright, intelligent, and credentialed, but rather to say that they did not serve him well because their sentiments often appeared at odds with the continental aspirations of Africa. For example, the operation against Gaddafi's Libya was universally condemned by Pan Africanists who saw Libya's role as the vanguard for the unity of the African continent. The killing of Gaddafi by forces allied to the United States was the bitterest pill for Africans to swallow in the two terms of Barack Obama.

So the criticism of Obama by progressive black and white critics has a lot to do with his use of drones that kill indiscriminately in Afghanistan, Iraq and Syria, and his use of AFRICOM to direct the American air war on African nations. Critics reserve, always, the harshest criticism for Obama's attacks on Libya, the country being the first to come under the American hammer. Regional alliances have been especially tricky for American African policies under the Obama Administration. The problem is that Obama's attempt to counter the al-Shabab and Boko Haram insurgents has created contradiction in America's policies and cracks in the alliances. Kenyan troops who invaded Somalia to pursue al-Shabab did so under the cover of Obama's American drones.

Obama's support for Kenyan soldiers who invaded Somalia to protect foreign tourists, Kenyan ports, and transportation routes from the attacks of Al-Shabab was a commitment to American military intelligence, not to Kenyan lives. Without showing favoritism to the country of his fathers's birth, Obama created the opportunity for expert engagement with the Kenyan government. Although Kenya's strategy has been to use Israel for heavy equipment, and specialized troops, the country has become America's best friend in East Africa. Probably since the terrorist attack on the American Embassy in Nairobi in 1998 the country has become one of the favorites of America foreign power wonks. In fact, Kenya has received nearly one billion dollars a year during the last few years of the Obama Administration.

Of course, clearly the American drones based at Kenya's Manda Bay facility and two bases in Ethiopia have cost even more money. When Ethiopia invaded Somalia in 2012 to attack al-Shabab it did so with the support of the Obama Administration. Earlier in 2006 Ethiopia had occupied Somalia for three years. With Obama's support Kenya and Ethiopia have played the role of America's hammer and anvil in East Africa. The Republican right wing prefers to see Obama's actions as those of a "foreigner and Muslim." There is almost nothing that Obama can do to appease this fringe element that lives on caravans of empty bags of racialized ideas.

No amount of American display of force in the world seems to appease the right wing. Even the African island nation of Seychelles has 100 U.S. troops and contractors servicing drones used over Somalia. Under the original U.S.–Seychelles agreement, drones were restricted to attacks on pirates but this has been expanded. Drones are the dominant American force in Somalia because after the Black Hawk Down incident we have not had boots on the ground in the country. If you ask me, however, the one area where Obama has been weakest is the African policy but the Right Wing could care less about Africa despite the fact that most of our platinum come from Namibia and Nigeria is rich in petroleum and oil, and other nations supply the United States and the West with many raw materials. Powerful interests in the United States have put their teeth deeply into the belly of Africa's resources and the Obama Administration has followed a policy of securing those American interests. As an Afrocentrist and Pan Africanist interested in seeing the economic and political rise of a continent that has been beaten down by the corporations and governments of the West I find the American agenda at odds with the best interests of the African people.

Clearly the United States' AFRICOM military base at Uganda's Entebbe airport is critical for U.S. military operations in the oil-rich Great Lakes region. When we first heard about this base it was to be the place where America would chase down the Lord's Resistance Army (LRA) that had created violent gangs that prevented access to the oil deposits.

The Lord's Resistance Army, a rag-tag group of nepotistic religious thugs, has moved into troubled South Sudan where more than 80 percent of Sudan's oil wealth is located. Major players are operating in South Sudan including the Chinese, the Sudanese, and other stakeholders including Uganda and the United States.

In West Africa, the United States has built a military base on the island nation of São Tomé and Príncipe. The base could be used to monitor any danger to resource rich West Africa, that is, any danger that could threaten the American pipeline of materials from West Africa. The announcement of the base was made in August 2002 and it has now become one of the place from which American troops are able to move up the West Coast of Africa. American troops are in Liberia, Senegal and Mauritania. While Obama did not start the military training of Nigerian soldiers or the war games with other African armies in the Gulf of Guinea, he nevertheless did not announce an understandable policy of neutralizing the Islamic Boko Haram religious gang.

One more concern seems to be the issue of Arabs versus Africans in Sudan. The second largest nation in Africa has exploded in racial violence where the Arabs are attacking the African people in a genocidal war in Nubia, Blue Nile, the Nuba mountains, and South Kordofan.

CHAPTER THREE

The Symbol of Mass Hope

Barack Obama campaigns for the presidency must be seen as culminating events in the largest national sense of optimism in the history of the nation. That is not to say that Obama fulfilled the dreams and hopes of a massive majority of Americans but his vision of a nation without the divisions of race, religion and politics was magnetic, particularly for an overwhelming number of African Americans. The idea is that no period in America's history was ever so full of optimism. If a nation could have been buoyed by the young dreams of a state politician anymore than the voters in the United States who sought the vision that was expressed in Obama's National Democratic Party's speech I have never read, seen or heard of such dreams. Here was the epitome of a nationalist vision of a heterogeneous nation arrayed in a multiplicity of political orientations and social angles. But what Obama's presidency would eventually reveal is the depth of the racism that still lurks in the inner soul of the American nation.

After the second election of the president all types of crude, lewd, and belligerent attacks were posted on the Internet challenging the mammoth amount of negativity presented to the media during the first campaign. In fact, Scott Walker, Governor of Wisconsin, who would eventually seek the Republican nomination to run to succeed Obama, even questioned whether Obama was a Christian. Walker's attack on the president was a frontal one as he claimed he did not believe what Obama had said about his religion. Whether Obama was an alien, Muslim, Jew, socialist, Kenyan native, communist, or Christian, his enemies were able to turn the optimistic tide in the country toward its gloomiest historical experiences where many black men were lynched primarily just for being black men.

There was some hope in the personal narrative of Obama that indisputably connected him to the dilemmas of the American nation in an existential manner. Who could avoid the African American with a white mother and an African father who carried within his body and soul the many doubts and possibilities of the typical American? In some ways Obama was the quintessential American despite the fact that during his first and second terms

The Symbol of Mass Hope

this would be criticized and attacked by the most vitriolic rhetoric ever launched against a presidential figure.

Barack Obama's 1994 memoir *Dreams from My Father: A Story of Race and Inheritance* contained all of the seeds of his promise and hope. He clearly demonstrates in keenly personal terms the complexities of identity in a white dominated society. For Obama to have been elected president of the *Harvard Law Review* as a student was itself a momentous achievement but his election to the presidency of the United States created animosities and tensions that he had never experienced at Harvard. Attacks on his vision of a promising future, especially around race, for the country he loved demonstrated the limitations of rhetorical dreams. Did others see what we saw as possible in a country that had gone through centuries of discrimination, 246 years of slavery, and more than a hundred years of Jim Crow, calls for affirmative action, and racial backlashes? Every opportunity he got to reflect on the question of identity and the dreams of a beautiful America where all people could exist in harmony, Obama related it to his family, both sides of his family. In fact, his Kansas and Kenyan sides are referenced in this quote:

> "I remembered the stories that my mother and her parents told me as a child, the stories of a family trying to explain itself. I recalled my first year as a community organizer in Chicago and my awkward steps toward manhood. I listened to my grandmother, sitting under a mango tree as she braid-

ed my sister's hair, describing the father I had never truly known" (*Dreams from My Father*, xiv).

Like his oratory Barack Obama's writing is inspired and richly textured although the issues he deals with are quite simple. He is a self-conscious writer inasmuch as he is a self-conscious politician. I think that this only means he was convinced that he would do something incredibly historical. One cannot read his books or study the trajectory of his life without knowing that he was profoundly committed to making his life matter. Always the burden of self-consciousness is to remain focused even when the odds do not appear in your favor. At the individual level this is different from the collective consciousness of the masses. Personally, as in his case, Obama could know and seemed to know precisely what was necessary to retain that symbol of hope that had become so complex in a people, the black people, who were looking and seeking "any sign" of a Moses, a Nat Turner, a new King, or an unknown, who could deliver the long awaited uncomplicated liberation for which our ancestors dreamed. If Obama mastered the technique of the dream, if he captured the rhetoric of the dream, it was because it seemed to be the prevalent trope among people who worshipped, prayed and talked about complete liberation like they were talking about the neighbor's new car.

Barack Obama became the face of the New Hope. He rode on the wings of the Dreamer and appeared like a messenger, to the deeply religious, sent from God from Heaven, to "bring the nation together." Of course, a dream is often the other side of the nightmare and there were others who saw him as "splitting the nation apart." Therein is the mystery of a man who brings both hope and despair, the summer breeze's and the winter's gale, while all the time self-consciously seeking to be the symbol that could create New Thought and New Practice of citizenship.

Thus, the African American population looked upon Obama's candidacy and his subsequent years in the White House in a prophetic sense. Obama had come not merely as a celebration of victory but more as a thorn in the side of racism because he had brought his intelligence, political acumen, and narrative of bi-raciality to the front of the line as evidence of his quintessential character as an American. Whose story could be any better? Who could claim to know the complexities of race and racial relations anymore than a child of a white mother and black father raised by white grandparents and acculturated by black people in churches and neighborhood centers in urban centers like Honolulu, Los Angeles, New York, and Chicago?

One must not forget that Reverend Jeremiah Wright was never a caricature in the African American community, but a teacher, a historian, a man of intense moral commitment to a society of restorative justice, and a devout culturalist in the African tradition. His religion had never been questioned and few equaled him in the nature of his hermeneutics or his social analysis. In 1995 Wright led a team of scholars including Cornel West and myself in an intensive training of 200 ministers at the United Theological Seminary in Dayton, Ohio. The topic was "Afrocentricity and Black Theology" and at the conclusion of the intensive there was a "debate" between West and myself. As the only person professing a belief in African religion I found myself defended in some respects by Jeremiah Wright who immediately understood my points although he was unashamedly Christian.

Wright served in the American military and later distinguished himself in the medical corps. He was educated at the best schools in the African American tradition and taught at colleges and seminaries. Jeremiah Wright was already an icon among black intellectuals when Barack Obama met him. Trinity Church had established itself as both Christian and Black, unapologetically. This is precisely the church that Barack Obama as a young professional and eventual politician chose to join in the Chicago community. Trinity Church of Christ was not pretentious; it was and probably remains a church with a mission of equality and liberation. Reverend Wright was Barack Obama's spiritual teacher.

Jeremiah Wright had preached an optimistic gospel without fear and shame and had brought together numerous intellectuals and scholars to outline the nature of the African past and to project the contours of a new future. He knew that the masses needed to sense hope and he was not a stranger to the narratives that brought Joe Louis, Jesse Owens, Jackie Robinson, Jack Johnson, or Muhammad Ali to the forefront of the nation. He wrestled with the compelling stories of courage found in Harriet Tubman, Sojourner Truth, Rosa Parks, and Fannie Lou Hamer and discovered symbols of hope that studded the history of African people in America. In fact, Obama's second book, *Audacity of Hope*, seemed to be inspired by Jeremiah Wright's sermon on the 'audacity to hope." Riffing off of a lecture by Dr. Frederick G. Sampson on a painting by G. F. Watts called *Hope* Wright had said "with her clothes in rags, her body scarred and bruised and bleeding, her harp all but destroyed and with only one string left, she had the audacity to make music and praise God.... To take the one string you have left and to have the audacity to hope... that's the real word God will have us hear from this passage and from Watt's painting." It appears that this may be the inspiration for *Audacity of Hope*.

Martin Luther King, Marcus Garvey, Nat Turner, Frederick Douglass, Booker T. Washington, and Malcolm X were symbols of hope in their own unique ways. Black people under duress looked endlessly for a deliverer. The myth of an African hero who would bring a dispensation of freedom, equality and justice had been planted deeply in the pit of black people's soul through long years of suffering oppressive conditions.

The election of Barack Obama thrust him into the role of a mass symbol for African people and it was this role that most aggravated many white Americans. The fear of a black president was palpable in the voice of many whites who were asked to comment on the election of Obama. Despite the fact that Obama deliberately and frequently reminded the nation that he was the President for the entire nation and that he was not interested in a "black America or a white America" the reality of his presence as President was one symbol too great for many whites to overcome. It was here, at this juncture, that the divide became greatest between blacks and whites in America because it was revealed how little whites, except a few of the more liberal ones, understood the character of African Americans among whom they lived. The idea of a liberator was too much for them to appreciate and hence all of the forerunners, Harriet Tubman, Nat Turner, Denmark Vesey, Frederick Douglass, Martin Luther King Jr., Malcolm X, and Kwame Ture could never be understood either. This part of our American history was invisible and silenced in the hearts of white people who were the descendants of the perpetrators of slavery or the inheritors of the privileges that accrued to whiteness by virtue of the enslavement. And since Obama was not directly descended, as far as we know, from enslaved Africans then this complicated his role even more in the minds of many white people. Why would he want to be the symbol of the masses of blacks? The question is irrelevant and Obama's answer would have been off-center because whether he liked it or wanted it or not did not matter. The only thing that mattered was that the African American community saw him coming in his shiny multicolored garments and held him up as a symbol of a collective victory, although one that could not have been won the 2008 race without the 43 percent of the white votes and the overwhelming majorities of black, Asian and Latino votes.

Ninety five percent of blacks voted for Obama; 67% of Hispanic voted for him; and 62% of Asians voted for Obama in the first election. McCain received 55% of all white votes.

In the second campaign of 2012 Obama received only 39% of the white vote while Mitt Romney received 59% of the white vote. Blacks went for Obama at 93%; Hispanics voted for Obama at 71% and Asians at 73%. Romney only received 6% of the African American vote. Consequently the nation was split deeply and badly and the fact that such a large portion of the white population, nearly 60%, did not want Obama to be president during the second campaign one could almost predict that he would have a rough legislative road to hoe. A recalcitrant Congress filled with anti-Obama congresspeople felt that they had lost their country because for the second time in as many elections a black man had won with a combination of Africans, Asians, Hispanics, and a strong core of liberal whites.

The Right Wing went nuts over the election for many reasons but certainly the idea that as a symbol of black conquest over discrimination and racism Obama would "disarm" whites by attacking their right to carry guns and somehow install blacks in control of all the reins of government. They had several persistent worries and concerns about a black man being in charge of the country for the second time. They thought that he would demonstrate weakness and show the world that the nation could not carry out its responsibilities. Obama proved to be a very astute politician and a capable world leader.

Obama as symbolic of black hope and optimism had started early in his campaign although he seemed not to notice. Even when he was elected, and had electrified the nation and impressed the world with his first presidential speeches, it was just enough to bring out the ugliest reactions on the part of the Obama haters. The *Atlantic* reported numerous vulgar and sick tweets flooded social media and bigots had a recreational period of attacks and assaults on the humanity of the newly elected President Barack Obama. To make him "damaged" goods was the purpose of a dedicated cadre of Obama haters. Of course, as usual in these situations, the South was particularly coarse in its assessment of Obama's first presidential election. Fueled by the biased radio and television pundits who predicted gloom with deafening booms bordering on hysteria, the Right Wing of American politics went into an uproar against the possibility of a black man occupying the White House. What would it mean and what would the world think about the United States? Of course, these were questions that came out of the ignorance of mistaken notions about the world. No presidential candidate had ever caused so much optimism as Obama and the entire world seemed to glory in his election. Millions of people were pleased, happy, and some of them thought that the United States had grown up in ways that European nations had not. France was especially struck by the recognition that America was not "as bad" as the French had thought.

When I went to Paris with my grandchildren in 2010 people

came up to me with smiles on their faces when they discovered we were from the United States. "America is a great country," they would say. Well, that is not what the Right Wing would have said. Their reaction was almost like nothing worse could have happened to the United States. Given the fact that blacks walked around proud of "their" country for making a reasonable selection in the election, many whites were sad. In fact, what blacks were happy about made whites cynical. Indeed, Michelle Obama said on one occasion during the election season she was proud of the United States of America and the right wing pundits jumped all over her. Why is she just proud now? They were adamant that she was speaking as if she disliked the United States, but here is what she actually said:

> "What we have learned over this year is that hope is making a comeback. It is making a comeback. And let me tell you something — for the first time in my adult lifetime, I am really proud of my country. And not just because Barack has done well, but because I think people are hungry for change. And I have been desperate to see our country moving in that direction and just not feeling so alone in my frustration and disappointment. I've seen people who are hungry to be unified around some basic common issues, and it's made me proud.?

Almost no African Americans saw anything troubling in this statement; we understood it profoundly and knew precisely what she meant because we felt what she felt. The reason she was not proud before was because it is difficult, almost insane, for black people to be proud of a nation that had practiced discrimination and brutality against blacks for so long. It was not a problem with most people who understood where she was coming from with the statement; but for others, anything that was said about the county had to be counteracted. White right wing true-believers looked for every reason and every way to damage Obama's presidential campaign.

The Right Wing saw Barack Obama in some regions of the country as an interloper, a mistake, an accident that happened when white supremacists were not as vigilant as they needed to be to protect their nation and so the social media outlets on the Internet blew up with vile, bitter, and obscene words, ads, and videos. In one of the most anti-intellectual moments white students at the stately University of Mississippi quickly assembled in a riot shouting racial slurs and negative terms of bigotry while tearing to shreds and burning Obama campaign materials when the voting seemed to be going his way. Some of the students posed with Confederate flags and sang "Dixie" and announced their disgust with the American voters who put him in office. Of course, they could have taken comfort in the fact that whites mostly voted for the opposition candidate.

CHAPTER FOUR

The Cradle of Abiding Fear

Rarely in the history of the presidency has an occupant been presented with such an array of domestic problems and issues as President Obama during the month of June 2015. At the same time the Supreme Court of the United States was deciding on the Affordable Care Act, the Fair Housing Law, and the legalization of Gay Marriage, President Obama was preparing to deliver a eulogy for the martyred South Carolinian pastor Clementa Pinckney and eight others killed in the Emanuel African Methodist Episcopal Church of Charleston, South Carolina. One is reminded of Ramses II's description of his desperate situation in the battle with Muwatalli II and the Hittites at Kadesh when he saw no way out because he was surrounded on all sides by his enemies with "no charioteers, no soldiers, and no shield bearer," but in the end Amen stood with him and he was able to extricate himself from the situation with grace.

Barack Obama's oratory at the funeral for State Senator and pastor Clementa Pinckney on June 25, 2017 rises to the highest levels of the American rhetorical tradition and places him alongside the greatest speakers in American history such as John Kennedy, Abraham Lincoln, Frederick Douglass, Ronald Reagan, and Martin Luther King Jr. The "Amazing Grace Speech" as it will be called was the crowning icon of his extremely brilliant presidential oratorical career. It was as much what he said as how he said it that distinguished this speech from all others that he had given on the subject of racism. "As a nation, out of this terrible tragedy, God has visited grace upon us for he has allowed us to see where we've been blind," Obama spoke with an emotion that had welled up in him for the years of his administration as he had to acknowledge the contradictions in the society he governed.

The stunning fact that the troubled and misguided shooter had entered a Christian church and mercilessly gunned down members of a spiritual prayer meeting circle gave the president once attacked for not being a Christian a chance to speak of what God had done to bring about grace. In fact, he said, "He's given us the chance, where we've been lost, to find our best selves." The theme of grace ran deep in the cadences of his speech and he hit the painful emotion of the confederate flag that had caused so much grief, dread, pain, and anguish by reminding those that hoisted that flag that removing it had nothing to do with the valor of their ancestors but the recognition that the cause for which they fought was wrong. A few days later Bree Newsome, an African American woman, climbed atop the South Carolina state building, and in an historic act of defiance, removed the Confederate Flag like she was cleansing the nation of an unholy stain. In some ways, inspired by Obama's attack on the Confederate flag, Bree Newsome brought a fitting end to a month fraught with dangers but yielding victories at every turn as Americans, blacks and whites, Asians and Latinos, recognized that the Civil War was over and that the South and its soldiers who fought and died gallantly had really lost the battle to defend the enslavement of Africans. No one has a right to absolute control over others and an any act of defiance is not only correct but should be expected by those who insist on maintaining a status quo that was indefensible.

Struck by criticisms on the Left and on the Right, saddened by the endless deaths of innocent people at the hands of a gun-toting society, overcome by the variety of oppressive measures that have sharpened the divisions in the country, the President sought to elevate his nation and to rally his people toward a belief in God's grace to help create what he always emphasized as "the United States of America."

It appears that guilt, shame and fear reside deep in the mind of some Americans because of the sins of enslavement and the crimes of discriminatory oppression. Seeking to keep African Americans inferior in their minds and in reality many white racists thought that by electing Barack Obama to the White House they would have lost their country. In a poignant punch line to this thinking Dylann Roof, frequently wrapped in the paraphernalia of the Confederacy, felt at the age of 21 that whites were losing their country. This muddled thinking is at the heart of America's "abiding fear." And yet many African Americans, descendants of those who fought to protect their freedom and the freedom of others, believe that this is their country as well despite the fact that Native Americans are clearly the only ones who can claim ownership.

The votarists of irrational race hatred who saw the election of Obama as a danger sign that the white population was losing its grip on American politics and leadership can only be called sad and unfortunate because these individuals were frightened of the potential of the United States of America to become a truly magnificent example of multicultural pluralism. Unable to explain the rise of Barack Obama in terms of the Constitution and the charters of rights and privileges of citizens the frighten had no other route but a rhetoric of fear. Its incessant tap-tap covered millions of conversations and added fuel to the already impotent-feeling people who would help to constitute the mob that would ceaselessly try to bring down the American president.

The Cradle of Abiding Fear

The brilliant African American essayist Ta-Nehesi Coates of the *Atlantic* has written, "As a candidate, Barack Obama said we needed to reckon with race and with America's original sin, slavery. But as our first black president, he has avoided mention of race almost entirely. In having to be "twice as good" and "half as black," Obama reveals the false promise and double standard of integration." Tapping into the polluted vein of fear running through Middle America Coates has placed his finger precisely on the spot that jerks the nation forward and sometimes backward. Fear, uncompromising fear of a black president, dogged the presidency during the first term of President Obama because so many whites did not know what would happen to them in an existential way. Some believed that they would have psychological collapse; others feared that the nation would break up into factions where vigilantes with machine guns would end up attacking the government. The insane fear of a black president by what appeared to be a majority of whites created lots of personal, political and professional crises for black-hating whites. As in the past when whites could not conceive of blacks working as their supervisors or socializing with whites or going to church with whites, now with the elections of Barack Obama they were faced with another fear: a black man with his hand on the nuclear war machine of the United States.

Their fear, it appears now, was linked to the same doctrine of white supremacy that was at the core of slavery, segregation, and discrimination. They did not believe that blacks were equal to whites in intelligence, reasoning, and judgment. How could a black man ever think that he could run any nation when all of the history of white supremacist teachings had said that there was never a nation run by blacks and that any nation run well in the ancient world that was in Africa, for example, Egypt or Nubia or Ethiopia, had to be because whites had infiltrated Africa and organized those societies? Strategies for Obama's defeat at least legislatively were put in place almost as soon as he was elected. Racists engaged in caucuses to see if they could "wait in the cut" for him to cross their path so that they could entrap him. Only time will tell, and others who worked with him, what other traps they laid for him to insure that the nation would not become satisfied that a black could in fact run any nation. Obama demonstrated during his first seven years that he was a clever politician, calm, not bellicose, intelligent without being arrogant, and quite capable in legal, domestic, and international matters.

Despite the fact that Obama "pitched his presidency as a monument to moderation" as Coates says, the Far Right Wing of American politics did not believe him. There must have been something in their own characters that produced such a wounded view of human possibilities. One wonders what they were expecting of the president. Did their fear have something to do with what they would have done in his place? Were they angry that a sizable group of liberal whites had overcome their own attachment to a racist society and voted for the best candidate? Nothing that Obama did could ease the agony that conflicted those who saw the strength of his character through various crises yet because of his African blood they would have none of him. They would have preferred Senator McCain or Governor Romney or any white, just not a black man. This was an accursed situation as far as the whites were concerned. Smartly Obama had poked the Reagan myth, the Lincoln myth, and the emerging Clinton myth as part of his armor.

Regardless to his cool, his intellect, his calm and deliberate way of generating along his political path quotes from Ronald Reagan, a darling of the Right-Wing, and Martin Luther King, Jr., the Civil Rights icon, and regardless to his olive branch approach to the Republicans in the House of Congress during his first term, and regardless to his avoidance of any sustained discourse on race, or his lack of playing the "race card" he was still a black man in a white man's seat as far as some of the fear-mongers thought. He did not allow any of the vile talk by riff-raff commentators or the unkind words and cartoons by obscenely malevolent critics to ruffle his neatly pressed look. He grew in stature and gravitas and they diminished themselves by the evil they spewed. His manners were impeccable and his dignity was intact. Therefore, more stunning than any thing he could have done in June 2015, Barack Obama in a national speech at the Arena of the College of Charleston in the heat of a June day came out of his shell, opened his mouth, took the form of his African American culture, and spewed forth the truth in a jeremiad that sounded as if he had seen Coates' assessment, studied the flowing periods of Douglass and King, Malcolm and Garvey, our greatest orators, and sang with graciousness his optimism that his nation would learn not simply the words but the work of an Amazing Grace.

The Southern Poverty Law Center says that the antigovernment so-called Patriot groups reached a high of 1360 groups in 2014. In fact, the number of hardcore racist groups with anti-Obama agendas has remained above 1000 during the President's entire term. Compare the number of "hate" groups in the white community with the three that the Southern Poverty Law Center counts in the African American community, the Nation of Islam, Nuwabeins, and the New Black Panthers, and it is not difficult to conclude that the white community's interest in such groups outstrips that in the black community. Indeed, some would argue that the three black groups are responses to white negativity and attacks on black people. However, my point is that the rage of the Right Wing is against Barack Obama and has been against him from the time that it appeared that he would be elected in 2008. After the first election racist materials directed toward the Head of State became a matter of concern. The number of race-hate fringe groups soared after Obama's election in 2008 and then again after the second election in 2012. The vile and obscene rhetoric of hatred flooded the Internet and found its way into the radio and television programs hosted by anti-Obama pundits who did not use the airwaves to teach and to quiet the rhetoric but rather to stir up as much venom as was possible and legal. The contempt as was spewed toward Barack Obama had never been seen against any presidential candidate or president in America's history.

After the 2012 election, and with the symbol of mass hope firmly entrenched in the traditional role of national leader, the Associated Press did a poll and discovered to the dismay of some that racial bigotry still lingers in most white Americans. Actually it was shown that 79 percent of Republicans and 32 percent of Democrats expressed hostility and negativity toward blacks in answers to the questions. What could have provoked such deeply troubling attitudes?

I remember saying to friends as I traveled to Asia, South America, Europe, and Africa to give lectures that most white voters did not vote for Obama. They were often stunned, wondering how could America have elected a black president and the majority of whites voted for John McCain during the first election and for Mitt Romney during the second election? Eric Ward explained the emerging progressive politics of the nation when he declared that "no Democratic candidate for the White House has won a majority of the white vote since the 1964 Civil Rights Act was passed by Democrats." In some ways, many whites, mostly Republican, but some Democrats, see the Democratic Party as a defender of the rights of others. They see the Civil Rights Act of

1964 as against white people. In their fear of mass democracy they will strike against all advances for blacks. They see these advances not in terms of human rights but in terms of white losses. There is at the heart of the fear of Obama a deep sadness that whites no longer can order the world to do their bidding without question.

I noticed a change in the attitudes whites had toward blacks in my own circle after the election. In fact, blacks shared with each other the negative reactions they felt or perceived after Obama was elected. It was like, Ok, so you have elected him but we will take it out on you in your local situation. The Southern Poverty Law Center says the number of race-hate fringe groups soared but it was more than the high number of fringe groups but it was the millions of slights, the attempts to disrupt routine business, and the rude assertion of advantage that most disturbed African Americans.

Of course, there are demographic differences. Young white voters tended to side with the progressive forces of the society. Older white voters tended to be less tolerant and more narrow-minded in their understanding of America. Racial diversity, multiculturalism, pluralism, and tolerance will have to be the mark of the new American. Whites are destined to be a numerical minority in the nation. Already Africans, Asians, Latinos, Pacific Islanders, and Native people comprise the largest number of students in public schools. It will be these Americans who will pay the bills and debts that will keep elderly white Americans alive.

The Cradle of Abiding Fear

The U.S. Census Bureau cannot be any more explicit that traditional European whites will be less than half of the population before 2040. In 2014 the number of white babies were below half of the babies born that year signaling the fact that the shift was already occurring in the nation. Massive numbers of "whites" or those who can be made "whites" will be required from an increasingly smaller pool of eligible people.

America is destined to become a browner nation. Mexican Americans will emerge as definitive political players in the West and other parts of the nation. Asian Americans are increasingly influencing local elections in a number of states. African Americans will continue to advance the progressive agenda for more human rights.

The great tension between tradition and innovation, between the past and the future, can be seen in the response to Obama's two terms. The Tea Party Republicans and their allies see Obama as expressing an aggressive Leftist agenda.

The *Charleston Gazette* (West Virginia) reported on November 15, 2012 that "Some scholars worry that white supremacy will remain in a different form–that affluent whites will continue wielding most wealth and power in America, even after they shrink below half of the population. That's an ugly picture, somewhat akin to South Africa."

What is clear, however, is that the numbers for African Americans and Latinos especially are increasing and it will become harder for the hard Right of the Republican Party to sustain itself with negative attacks on blacks and Latinos. Obama's election on two occasions showed the society that the future would be different from the past and most of the attacks on Obama are a result of political fear. Although it is an irrational fear; it is the fear of imminent loss. Obama is seen as an alien in the world that has been dominated by whites since the beginning of the nation. Millions of dollars were spent during the first Obama campaign to prevent him from beating John McCain. The Republicans brought all of their giant killers to the political arena and the one of the best at that time was a consultant named Karl Rove. However, even Rove had no answers for the profound way that Obama touched the chord of the American public. It was left to columnists and pundits to comment on the decline of Rove's power and the actual defeat of the experts by the Obama machine. For example, Walter Hickey wrote an article in *Business Insider* on November 6, 2012 that claimed "Karl Rove's Historically Colossal Waste Of Money" did not end in the defeat of Barack Obama although more than 80 million dollars was raised and more than 100 million dollars spent by his American Crossroads Super Pac.

The ex-Governor of Pennsylvania and former Democratic National Committee chair, Ed Rendell, said during the 2008 election that there were some whites that wouldn't vote for a black man. This astonished some people but he was being realistic given the nature of racial animus in the nation. When the

University of Texas at Austin's campus could have massive statues of Confederate leaders such as Jefferson Davis and Robert E. Lee on its campus for 80 years one can assume that there is still in America, especially in the Deep South, but increasingly throughout the nation, people who truly believe that the enslavement of Africans was a good thing. To see a descendant of an African in the White House when they would never place a statue of him on the lawn of the University of Texas must have irritated those who wrote and spoke with such venom against the President of the United States.

Anger and antagonism against Obama followed him after the campaign into the White House where he walked a sensitive social tightrope knowing the character of his nation, but probably not so well as he would have had he grown up in the South and been schooled by the endemic racism of southern whites. As the late New Orleans' culturalist Morris Jeff said and the Def Jam poet Sunni Patterson expresses so vividly "We know this place." The American South has always had special lessons to teach about racism. So Obama was careful, almost to a fault, not to speak too much on race and rarely on racism. I remember when Trayvon Martin was killed in Sanford, Florida, that the President reflected on the situation and spoke on the condition of black children in the nation especially in places where black boys are often racially profiled:

> "When I think about this boy, I think about my own kids, and I think every parent in America should be able to un-

derstand why it is absolutely imperative that we investigate every aspect of this, and that everybody pulls together—federal, state, and local—to figure out exactly how this tragedy happened ....

But my main message is to the parents of Trayvon Martin. If I had a son, he'd look like Trayvon. I think they are right to expect that all of us as Americans are going to take this with the seriousness it deserves, and that we're going to get to the bottom of exactly what happened."

Obama's statement was both presidential and personal. He demonstrated leadership by stepping into the national pain and then he spoke personally about his own children. Ta-Nehesi Coates has written cogently in "Fear of a Black President" that "The moment Obama spoke, the case of Trayvon Martin passed out of its national-mourning phase and lapsed into something darker and more familiar—racialized political fodder. The illusion of consensus crumbled. Rush Limbaugh denounced Obama's claim of empathy. *The Daily Caller*, a conservative Web site, broadcast all of Martin's tweets, the most loutish of which revealed him to have committed the unpardonable sin of speaking like a 17-year-old boy. A white-supremacist site called *Stormfront* produced a photo of Martin with pants sagging, flipping the bird. *Business Insider* posted the photograph and took it down without apology when it was revealed to be a fake" (Ta-Nehesi Coates, *The Atlantic*, August 22, 2012)

Coates captured the deafening noise of racial chatter underlining the fear felt by the Right-Winging whites whose only ambition was to defeat the president. President Obama attempted by his comments to filter all of the noise and restore a sense of common purpose to the nation. Many whites could care less about common cause or purpose with black Americans or with an African American president. The critical issue for white Americans, at least, the racists who believed in white supremacy, was how to combat the unexpected rise of what Martin Luther King saw as inevitable, a black president. The rise of Obama introduced a crisis in the maintenance of a form of white institutional control and intensified the struggle to assert white dominance, even over a black president.

We know, as I have demonstrated, that even before Obama was elected the first time, there were already negative reactions to him. For example the *Christian Science Monitor* reported in 2008, "Sonia Whittle is a Mexican-American married to a white Republican man. She often picks up the scuttlebutt on the streets of Forest Park, a largely black and Hispanic neighborhood in Georgia. Because of her Hispanic appearance, whites and blacks often think she doesn't speak English, so she overhears racial prejudices from all three populations." We are not told precisely what Whittle hears whites, blacks, or Hispanes say. To say that Whittle "overhears racial prejudice" might be stretching it too far when it comes to African American people. I personally do not see how the character of remarks by African Americans in this chronological frame could have been placed in the same category as racial remarks by whites. Here is the problem. I believe that blacks may have spoken of whites but certainly not in derogatory terms or in the sense of denying rights and privileges of citizenship to them because of their race, and certainly not attacking the president. The point is one can speak of race and racism and not be making a racist comment. However, when racist talk dominates conversation and racial innuendoes that are negative and poisoning occupy time on the radio, the Internet, or the newspapers then we are at another level of discourse. Therefore, Whittle could say something like "I hear this [racial] stuff every day – it's real," and be expressing what she actually believes to be the most dominant conversation in her reality. However, when she says. "I think a lot of whites are afraid of what's going to happen if Obama gets elected. Everybody's real confused right now" she is stating an opinion based on what she perceives to be a racist commentary. It was as if whites could not even see the possibility of a sane society if Obama were elected. So fearful were some Republicans that they tried all types of techniques to poison the political atmosphere. For example, in Tampa, Florida the leader of the Hillsborough County Republican Party sent an e-mail warning whites of "the threat of carloads of black Obama supporters coming from the inner city to cast their votes" in 2008. David Storck, the Republican, leader was called a racist and was forced to resign once the email he forwarded was discovered. Ron Whitley, a 72 year old Republican had sent the email written in all capital letters to Storck who then forwarded it to 400 Republicans. The email began with the title "The Threat," and then announced that Whitley saw these "carloads of black Obama supporters" from the inner city coming to cast their votes for Obama. He writes that "this is their chance to get a black president and they seem to care little that he is at minimum, socialist, and probably Marxist in his core beliefs. After all, he is black—no experience or accomplishments—but he is black."

Storck prefaced his forwarding of the e-mail by saying: "If you think it can help us win this election, please pass it on." Clearly what was going on in this email was an attempt to frighten white voters into going to the polls. It was called racist by Curtis Stokes, the leader of the Hillsborough County Chapter of the NAACP who was also a member of the county Republican Party. The idea that a black person might become president was enough to strike fear into the heart of whites. Yet probably because Stokes was a member of the GOP the party condemned the rhetoric of the emails.

In a similar vein the elusive Porter Stansbury warned that Obama would become "a tyrant" because what happened in 2008 would radically shape the country and "enable the president to implement the most socialist government" (See http://pro.stansberryresearch.com/121....).

So here was the situation that Obama was facing in 2008: his presidential election, as far as whites were concerned had to do with their own sense of security. They were afraid but their fright had a lot to do with their notion of *"what's going to happen"* if he were elected. We know that what happened when Obama was elected was that some whites, led by reactionary forces in the Congress, decided that he could not be successful. In fact they vowed to insure that he not be successful. The strategy of uncompromising fear was that whites must insure that he not be elected and if for some reason he were elected they must insure that he not be successful. A successful African American president, with intelligence, talent, and energy, would defeat all racist stereotypes and ideologies for a long time. Thus, when Sonia Whittle first spoke about the situation in 2008 she was clear that the country was "not ready" for a black president.

Readiness in terms of racial or social justice always borders on obscenity because the verbal arsenal of Right-Wingers contains cannons of readiness that are abusive, arrogant, and applied only to the emergence of justice. Who is to dictate when a society is "ready" for justice, equality, or the election of a black president? Surely this cannot be left to those who would, if they could, never permit power to be shared. We see the same arsenal applied when it comes to voting rights. The idea is to make it difficult for blacks or Hispanics to exercise their rights to vote especially if those votes would support progressive candidates. Fortunately not all of the people followed the lead of the circle around Sonia Whittle and Barack Obama won the election; this means that enough people were ready for the election of whomever they thought was the better candidate. African Americans and some liberal whites, Asians, and Latinos seemed to worry what would happen in American communities or between the races if Obama *did not* win. ("Surging Obama campaign suggests US racism on the wane" Alexandra Marks, Staff WriterCopyright *The Christian Science Monitor* Oct 23, 2008)

CHAPTER FIVE

The Denial of Authenticity

A major part of the lynching of Obama is the denial of his Americanness. In effect, the deniers claim that Obama is not like they are and that he might even be anti-American. The fact that he was a Senator from Illinois did not matter. The fact that he was educated in the United States with all of his degrees from outstanding American universities did not matter. The only thing that mattered to the Obama haters was the fact that he was a black man. As the *other* he was a perfect person to be verbally abused and lynched in the press and on the platform throughout the country. Their delusion that their problems had to do with blacks, Muslims, Jews, Hispanics, or Asians rested on the old rock of white racial domination. Obama's presence challenged all delusions because he was not a commodity that could be readily swallowed.

Glenn Beck told his audiences that what they thought they knew about Obama was "nothing but fiction." Beck said that the man "who sits behind the desk in the oval office" is the most powerful man in the world. "He is our representative and he is not like us. He is our representative." It irks him that Obama as President of the United States is not like him. (https://www.youtube.com/watch?v=yQLdPTXeapg). Rupert Murdoch, Beck's conservative boss, and owner of Fox News, insulted the President with an October 2015 tweet in support of the conservative Republican candidate Ben Carson when he wrote that it was time to have "a real black person in the White House." Of course, Murdoch supposes that he knows more than black people who the real black person is.

The Right-Wing idea that Obama was not American stung him and his supporters as one of the most un-American things that his enemies could say. Even when the Hawaiian authorities presented his birth certificate there was a controversy over its presentation. Michael Huckabee, former Arkansas governor, running for the Republican nomination for president in 2015 said "Obama does like Christians or Jews and the only people he likes are Muslims" (*Daily Mail*, February 9, 2015). This was a lie but it received wide circulation in the conservative circle. In fact, Obama had spoken at the National Prayer Breakfast the week before and had criticized the Muslim dominated ISIL group but had also spoken about the Crusades led by Christians for several hundred years. Perhaps the inability of Right-Wingers to accept any lessons about negative actions by whites constitutes the basis of their criticism. Donald Trump, who would run for the Republican nomination for the presidency in 2016, took up the assault on Muslims and ran with Huckabee's entry right into the core of American bigotry. Thus, in December 2015, Trump insisted that he would keep all Muslims out of the United States. There had been enough said by him and other Republican candidates for the nomination of their party about Obama's unwillingness to use certain words about Muslims to create the idea that Obama was for Muslims and against Christians.

The attack on Obama's authenticity had many sides; however, the most telling aspect of it was the fact that it showed that the Right-Wing wanted to divest him of any claim to American identity. But there was a more subtle part to the attack: they did not and could not see Obama, despite his white mother, to see him as a white person. Of course, the American notion of race revolved around the one-drop rule where one drop of African blood made a person African. Secondly, conservatives who sought to undermine his nationality challenged Obama's Hawaiian birth records. The birth certificate attack was truly ridiculous when you consider it thoroughly. After the Tea Party enthusiasts made their declarations about the lack of a birth certificate Donald Trump, not known for intellectual brilliance, a billionaire, jumped on board the same train. During his first run for the Presidency, Obama had his team produce many copies of his birth certificate and distribute them to the press but many were not impressed. He never concentrated on defending his citizenship often dismissing the questions out of hand. This served to aggravate the "birthers," who wanted to know if he was born in the United States and if his document of birth is authentic.

When the partisans sought to get the courts involved in the question of Obama's birth certificate the legal system relied on

Barack Obama's White House Released Birth Certificate

The Denial of Authenticity

ideas like "standing," that is, whether an individual can bring such a lawsuit without demonstrating "harm," or "injury" should Obama occupy the White House. They were never able to show such injury by Obama's presidency. However, their claims were interesting, given the fact that they had lost in the voting process, and Obama would become the first black president, they used all of the machinations in their arsenal of gutter politics. They said that he was born in Indonesia. Others said he was born in Kenya. Still more thoughtful "birthers" agreed that he was born in Hawaii but that he had dual American and British citizenship because his father was a Kenyan and Kenya was a British colony. Others were even more confused and could not understand anything about his birth. In fact, a white member of the Hawaii state government complicated the situation with his opinion. member of the Hawaii State Senate said today he believes Barack Obama is not releasing his long-form birth certificate because he may want to hide the identity or citizenship of his father.

In an extraordinary attack and questionable assault, Republican Sam Slom, said he believed Obama wanted to hide something about his birth. He is quoted as saying, "My particular point of view... is that he probably was born in Hawaii and that the real issue is not the birth certificate, but what's on the birth certificate" (Interview on New York's WABC 770 AM radio station, December 2011). Slom's suspicion was that Obama wanted to hide his father's citizenship although that would not have prevented Obama from being an American citizen since he was born to Ann Dunham in Honolulu.

The birthers were adamant that he was not American.

Once he decided to run for the presidency, though before he had announced, Donald Trump added his loud voice to the assault on Obama. Trump repeatedly questioned Obama's eligibility to serve as president although Trump had no qualifications or credentials for being president.

The facts of Obama's biography are quite clear in that Barack Obama's mother Stanley Ann Dunham met the President's father, Barack Obama, Sr., in a Russian class at the University of Hawaii in 1960. He had come from Nyang'oma Kogelo, Kenya as the first African student at the university.

He was 23 years old and very intelligent. He married Ann Dunham on February 1961 in Maui when Dunham was already three months pregnant with Barack who was born on August 4, 1961. His name appears in the Hawaii State government binder for computer generated birth index from 1960-1964 as Barack Hussain Obama II. This is found in the Honolulu State Department of Health. Barack's parents divorced in January 1963.

Trump nevertheless in 2011 called the Obama birth certificate situation "one of the greatest cons in the history of politics and beyond." Trump's rhetoric can be called racist and bigoted but mostly it is ignorant and ranty, sort of the worst aspects of the nasty white supremacist. All one has to do is to examine the numerous comments he has made regarding other people, Mexicans, Chinese, or Muslims, and you can see that he has the most gall to actually verbalize the hatred and fear felt by whites who seem to respond to a siege mentality. He is a demagogue who has played on the emotions of people who are trying to sort out their lives in a shifting world where whites will no longer be able to have the privileges over other people that they have held for many years.

Donald Trump remains one of the biggest agnostics about Obama's authenticity. In what would predict the vile tone of his own presidential run, Donald John Trump said of Barack Obama, "The people that went to school with (Barack Obama), they never saw him, they don't know who he is."(*Politifact*, February 14, 2011). Of course, this was not true. In fact, one of Obama's young class mates sent this photo of the two of them.

Barack Obama with a third grade friend in Manoa

Trump's own ancestors came to the United States from Germany and Scotland during the late 19th century and early 20th century. His grandfather, Friederich Christ Trump, immigrated from Kallstadt, Pfalz, Germany, in 1885 and started a business in British Columbia. He later became an American citizen in Seattle, Washington in 1892. Trump's father, Frederick Christ Trump, was born in New York. His mother, Mary Anne McLeod, was born on the Isle of Lewis, Scotland, in 1912.

Trump is a third-generation American on his father's side and a second generation on this Scottish mother's side. Obama, on his mother's side, has deeper roots in America than does Trump.

Trump led people like Sarah Palin, who actually did not need leadership in stupid things to say, to also assault the president's birth certificate. While Trump's ignorance was on display all over the place with statements about having people "studying" who cannot believe "what they're finding" about Obama's birth certificate to "there are no photos of him as a young person, only when he was a teenager." These were groundless lies but what Trump understood as a demagogue is that you do not have to defend your lies, you go on to the next one is you want to demonstrate to the masses that you have the courage to express their inner thoughts. What Trump has his finger on is the beliefs and wishes of a small minority of whites who are searching for some reason to claim that Obama is faulty, broken, unreal, inauthentic, but what he ends up doing is to expose himself as someone who lacks morality

The Denial of Authenticity

and authenticity. He is the fake that he is looking for in the president; this is burden. Everything he does against President Obama displays his own inner fears.

Sarah Palin climbed aboard the birther's wagon by claiming that there is "something that the president doesn't want people to see, that he seems to be going to great lengths to make sure it isn't shown." As we know there was nothing in these attacks that were sustained by history, facts, or the record keeping of the Hawaiian State government. Barack Hussain Obama is an American born citizen.

The Right-Wing could not find any footing anywhere that would give them a location from which to attack Obama's citizenship. Authorities in Hawaii, hospital executives and newspaper editors, indicated that he was born in Hawaii. Yet the Right Wing Tea Partyers had the idea that Obama or his mother must have known that he would run for the presidency so they had falsified his records, and perhaps the birth certificate was a forgery. Every stratagem possible was used to create the ropes upon which they intended to hang the president. But as the saying is about Shaka, the Great, leader of the Zulu Nation in the 19th century, the "women gossiped at the wells that Shaka would never be king, but as they gossiped he was already entering the third year of his reign." Obama quietly went on with presidency rarely distracted by the noise surrounding him.

The white politicians from the Right did not know how to

accept the new president. They broke all protocols of propriety when it came to Barack Obama. Within a years after he had been elected Joe Wilson, a Republican Representative from South Carolina, the first Confederate State, was so full of venom during the President's speech to Congress on health care that he blurted out loudly while the President was talking, "You lie!" when the President was denying that the health care plan would cover illegal immigrants.

I remember thinking that the disrespect shown the office of the Presidency of the most powerful nation in the world was atrocious and totally out of bounds. Some people thought that he had planned the outburst and others thought that it was spontaneous. Wilson's yell made him appear like the jerk in the Congress but other people in the nation probably shared Wilson's sentiments. Some people saw him as a hero.

The Republican leadership soon cajoled Wilson to apologize to the White House. The fact that the comments were inappropriate was only one issue; the other was that the CNN review of the Congressional Research Service said: "the proposal clearly says that federal subsidies would go only to U. S. citizens and immigrants who are in the United States legally." Being the person he had been trained to be the President accepted the apology and made such an announcement to his Cabinet the next day.

However, it should be pointed out that Representative Louie Gohmert, R-Texas, had a sign around his neck at the same speech criticizing the health care bill. Senator McCain, a former Republican presidential candidate, said that Wilson's outburst was totally disrespectful. What the Republicans who made inappropriate remarks and protests forgot was that the Presidency is greater than the person in the office. The House Whip at the time was the African American Jim Clyburn, D-South Carolina, and he said, "I was always taught that the first sign of a good education is good manners. I think that what we saw tonight was really bad manners." Clyburn was clear in his statement and he knew that what the Right Wing politicians had done was to insult the Presidency and when you insult the Presidency you are actually insulting the nation, the high office of the Commander-in-Chief.

In 2015 when John Boehner invited Benjamin Netanyahu of Israel to give a speech to the Congress without the protocol of consulting the Presidency he was essentially doing the same thing, insulting the nation. The fact that a foreign President took the invitation without consulting with the Chief Executive of the United States was also an insult. Furthermore, Boehner may have been flirting with violation of the Logan Act.

After giving his sixth state of the nation speech where he had promised to veto any legislation against the Iran deal Obama waited for the Republicans to act. Boehner reacted by the invitation to Netanyahu and in so doing violated nearly three hundred years of political protocol between the Congress and the Presidency. More directly Boehner may have violated the Logan

Act created in 1799 to prevent individuals from acting on their own in international affairs. The Logan Act clearly indicates that it a federal crime punishable by prison when Americans without authorization negotiate on behalf of the American government. It states:

> Any citizen of the United States, wherever he may be, who, without authority of the United States, directly or indirectly commences or carries on any correspondence or intercourse with any foreign government or any officer or agent thereof, with intent to influence the measures or conduct of any foreign government or of any officer or agent thereof, in relation to any disputes or controversies with the United States, or to defeat the measures of the United States, shall be fined under this title or imprisoned not more than three years, or both.
>
> This section shall not abridge the right of a citizen to apply himself, or his agent, to any foreign government, or the agents thereof, for redress of any injury which he may have sustained from such government or any of its agents or subjects.

Clearly Boehner wanted to bring the Israeli President into the Congress with intent to influence the measures or conduct of a foreign government.

Some have even argued that Boehner may have violated the Federal Elections Commission (FEC) law, section 441e, because it states that "it shall be unlawful for a foreign national, directly or indirectly, to make a contribution or donation of money or other thing of value, or to make an express or implied promise to make a contribution or donation, in connection with a Federal, State, or local election...." While Netanyahu did not offer any cash to the Republicans he did offer them something that might be called "a thing of value" because his speech allowed the Republicans to raise more money from Israeli supporters and for other fundraising activities. Instead of investigating whether of not Obama is a natural born citizen the Republicans could have examined Boehner's possible violation of laws and protocol.

Of course, it was not just Republicans who questioned whether or not Obama could be President. Even when Obama was running for the Presidency during the first term, Hillary Clinton, who would later work with Obama, resorted to the idea of inauthenticity. Rhodes E. Washington wrote in the *Philadelphia Tribune*, April 25, 2008 that "When Clinton says Obama is unelectable and the "Eurostream" media says Obama can't close the deal, you can be sure the phrase "working class whites" is lurking nearby, whether it is said aloud or not." Rhodes knew that the code words and terms used by politicians to manipulate the masses of ignorant white voters were being used by all of Obama's challengers. Why would he be "unelectable"? What was the meaning of this term in the context of the electorate if it was not meant to insinuate that his race made him un-electable. Perhaps Hillary Clinton knew something about the white population and its response to blackness that we did not want to accept.

This idea of Barack Obama's inauthenticity would not vanish simply because he was elected to the presidency. It was a meme that found its strength in the composition of the American white electorate. Fear of a black United States president was so palpable that the Right Wing fringe movement used every conceivable tool to stop Obama's election and even after he was elected twice the birthers did not relent in their irrational cry that he was inauthentic.

This is such a potato trying to be a mango. In fact, the majority of whites in the United States cannot trace their heritage past four generations. On the other hand, the majority of Africans in this country have been in the country for six or seven generations. That fact does not prevent racists from accusing Michelle Obama of not being sufficiently loyal to the United States.

Just a statement that she was truly proud of her country for its phenomenal outpouring of interracial action to elect Barack Obama she was condemned by the conservatives. There is certainly nothing wrong with the penned up emotions of a black person bursting forth in a joy that had been awaited for nearly three hundred years. Michelle Obama, on that occasion, may not have stirred the emotions of white immigrant families, but she got to the soul of the African American population. Not even the meanness of the Right Wing commenting on her looks, style, and gender could distract the masses of liberal, progressive black and white people from their love of Michelle.

Perhaps the most haunting image of meanness is the way Michelle Obama was attacked in the early days of the first term. The First Lady had her own exceptional career path before she met Barack Obama. She was a graduate of Princeton and Harvard, had taken courses in African American Studies, knew something about her own history, personally and collective, in the United States. As a University Hospital Administrator and a lawyer with outstanding insight into the law herself she was not a wallflower and would not nor could ever be a woman simply darting around the White House with fluffy dreams. She was and indeed is a significant person in her own right. This is one reason the vile video expressing the opinion that she was a "man" became one of the most enduring images of meanness. For me, the irony is that she was the First Lady of the Nation to which the mean-spirited individual or individuals belonged. What would make you believe that your national First Lady was something other than what her history, career, genetics, and family life said she was? The only thing I can think of is some primordial or Neanderthalian notion that she was not worthy to be considered the First Lady because of her complexion and overpowering beauty as a woman. But it is the same attack that the president has suffered at the hands of the Right Wing. Meanness is not the same thing as a difference of opinion about concepts, behaviors and actions; it is a nasty and irrational attitude toward other people. In the case of the President and the First Lady this computed as dislike for the reality of a black family occupying the White House. Anything they did was looked upon as negative in the eyes of those who felt that the Ku Klux Klan should have been called in to threaten black people.

But there is also a lowdown political quality to the manipulation of white voters' attitudes that shows these attackers have little regard for the intelligence of their white voters. For example, we know that the dog whistle campaign of 2008 sought to show Barack Obama darker than he actually is to frighten whites who were believed to be more emotional the blacker the person. Public Opinion published new evidence that this was the case in December 2015. Analyzing 126 advertisements from the campaign researchers digitally measured the darkness of the two nominees' skin in each spot then sorted the ads into categories based on various themes. Of course, Sen. John McCain (R-Ariz.) appeared different depending on how the footage was edited. Accordingly when McCain's campaign tried to connect Obama with alleged criminal activity by liberals, the producers almost always made Obama's skin tone darker. Videos were even used in the attempt to demonstrate that Obama was not really an American.

There was a video made soon after the first Obama election that purported to have him say that he was not an American citizen. Regardless to how bizarre this sounds and how really odd it is that a trained Constitutional lawyer from Harvard University, a University of Chicago Law Professor, and someone who knows the Constitution, and indeed was a sitting president at the time he was supposed to say that he was ineligible to hold the office, there are some people who still believe that President Obama said "I am not an American. I was not born in Hawaii and I was not born in the United States of America." One wonders how something called "Not Born in America: Truth Matters" gets made and distributed with the instruction "Circulate this before they yank it off the Internet." From both an ethical and a practical perspective this was pure bunk but the readiness to believe that Obama was not a natural born American citizen was at the core an impossible racist wish.

CHAPTER SIX

Demanding Guilt

Mobs demand guilt even of the guiltless. In the case of the Right Wing assault on Barack Obama the set up was to color him with a brush of association that would show that he was either a socialist or a black nationalist. In either case he would demonstrate that he was unfit for the presidency in the eyes of the Republican Right. Of course, early on in the media confusion surrounding the early biography of Barack Obama some liberals were also coaxed into making crude mistakes. The *New Yorker Magazine*, for example, published a front-page picture depicting a fist-thumping Michelle Obama looking at Barack dressed in a fez and a robe. The public immediately responded to the image many thinking that it adequately depicted the religion and the self-assertion of an anti-American Obama. His campaign was angry, the conservatives rejoiced in a craven acceptance of the front cover as showing the real Obama. The editor of the *New Yorker* explained that the front cover was to depict the manipulation of the Rith Wing in suggesting the Obamas were not Americans. However, many people missed the satire and some conservatives referred to the information on the cover as a real image of the Obama persona.

For the enemies of Obama, he had to admit guilt or at least say that he was wrong to be a radical socialist, Muslim, or Black Nationalist, ideas that he never expressed as a candidate. (http://www.youtube.com/watch?v=AHlxhiyCBL8).

During Obama's campaign and presidency there would be certain behaviors that would cast doubt in the minds of reactionaries. Did you see him whisper to Putin, the President of Russia, saying that he would have to wait until the election was over? Did you know that he was really associated with wildly liberal people such as Bill Ayers and Molefi Kete Asante? There was nothing that those demanding guilt of the president would not do to prove their point. They would stick Obama with association glue to force guilt.

For instance, the reactionary Jack Cashill claims to have demonstrated that in Obama's book *Dreams from My Father* the candidate Obama pays homage to me. As an educator and writer I have said many things about the injustice, inequality and brutality in this society and none of them have been seditious or treasonous or untrue as far as I know. What Cashill claimed in September 2008 was that Obama's memoir, *Dreams From My Father*, had certain passages that really sounded like Molefi Kete Asante. He writes in June 2009 on his blog, *American Thinker* "The tip-off once again is the contrived name, in this case "Asante Moran," likely an homage to the Afro-centric educator, Molefi Kete Asante. Moran lectures Obama and his pal "Johnny" on the nature of public education." Cashill attributes this entire section to the influence of the brilliant educator Bill Ayers whose history of social protest rattles Cashill's brain. Furthermore, he says that this character, Asante Moran, says, "The first thing you have to realize," he said, looking at Johnnie and me in turn, "is that the public school system is not about educating black children. Never has been. Inner-city schools are about social control. Period."

Apparently to seal his case that *Dreams from my Fath*er had the imprint of Bill Ayers and Molefi Kete Asante, Cashill writes "In *Dreams*, "Moran" elaborates on the fate of the black student, "From day one, what's he learning about? Someone else's history. Someone else's culture. Not only that, this culture he's supposed to learn is the same culture that's systematically rejected him, denied his humanity." If Obama meant to include my words and ideas in his memoir, I am flattered by the relevance he found in those words. However, there is no evidence that I have that this was the case. In fact, I know several other individuals who have and would have made the same statements about education. My record on this subject is quite public and I believe that there is nothing out of the ordinary conversationally for a character living in contemporary urban America to make such a statement about education. This is the reality. Cashill is looking to smear Obama and in the end exposes the nature of American racism. His entire blog list reads like a mean-spirited drunk whose ambition is to make everyone else drunk on his madness about Obama. What he has for Bill Ayers, the distinguished professor of education, is even worst because he sees Bill Ayers, who is a very kindhearted individual, as the bogeyman behind Barack Obama.

Thus, Hillary Clinton's supporters may have spread the original suspicion about Obama's birth but she later renounced the claims of the birthers. Nevertheless, the usual Right-Wingers disputed the evidence suggesting that they were wrong and plowed ahead into the rocky soil of demanding guilt of the accused. I am sure that the aim of the rhetoric demanding that the president, and even when he was a candidate, admit some sort of guilt it was because of the deeply held racist beliefs that he was not "one of us" and that despite his mother "he was still black." In fact, some really fringe writers went so far as to claim that Obama was the child of his white grandfather and a black prostitute. Who comes up with this type of wishful biological talk but racists? Who would want to believe this sort of talk? Another scenario says that Obama is the child of a black communist and his mother Ann Dunham. The key here is that the Obama-haters really want to show that he is not, indeed cannot be, a real black man and be president.

The evidence that Barack Obama is a natural-born U.S. citizen is so overwhelming that disputing this fact constitutes a form of venal denialism, rather than a mere conspiracy theory. As his birth certificate showed, the President was born in Honolulu, Hawaii, at Kapiolani Hospital, on August 4, 1961,the child of an immigrant Kenyan father (Barack Obama, Sr.) and American mother (S. Anne Dunham). Yet the smears continued and finally the Obama campaign created a website called *Fight The Smears* which showed a short form of Obama's birth certificate. Obama also allowed factcheck.org to distribute information about his birth. Some conservatives said this was not enough. The State of Hawaii then came out with the long form of Obama's birth certificate just before Election Day in 2008 as an indication that Obama was born in Hawaii and was thus a natural-born citizen as required by the Constitution.

Linked to all of the other birther insanity about Barack Hussein Obama was the argument that he was actually Osama Bin Laden. Millions of people viewed a video that made the case for claiming that the 6'1 Obama was actually the 6'5 Bin Laden. Later when Osama Bin Laden was killed by orders of Barack Obama the reactionaries had no answer for the man who was supposed to have killed himself! The paranoid that gripped the first Obama run for the presidency did not end with his re-election to a second term. Fierce Obama hatred drove over 7 million Americans and others to view a video claiming that Obama was Osama. Many of them actually believed that Al Qaeda had infiltrated the American political system and elected one of their own as President of the United States of America! Thus, the American born president was transformed several times in the words and language of the conservatives. They claimed that he was Kenyan, Indonesian, Jewish, Muslim, gay, or Osama Bin Laden. A combination of craziness affected the Obama-hating crowd who would not tolerate rational thinking and whose critical thinking capacity ended with Obama being a part of some giant "reptilian illuminati Bilderberg trilateral commission" conspiracy to take down America. According to them, Obama is a terrorist who seeks to weaken the destroy the economy, encouraged America's enemies, remove all guns from individuals, and discouraged America's allies. Some Obama haters went so far as to claim that Ronald Reagan, the prophet of the extreme white Republican fringe, warned about the coming of Obama. Hatred for anyone who claimed to have read and studied the literature of the left was so deeply ingrained in the rhetorical soul of the extreme right that any voice that was uttered against President Obama seemed eerily to reflect a madness of thought.

Not only was the candidate Barack Obama the "Teflon candidate," however, he proved to be the "Teflon" president. His attention to duty and his command of the political process were evidences of a superior knowledge of the Constitution and the demands of being the leader of the democratic world.

I have always found that some of the most ignorant people are those expressing religion. This is not to condemn all religious people or to say that non-religious people are always smarter but rather to point to a peculiar relationship between the church and race in the American society. Perhaps this is due to the history of the church's involvement with the European Slave Trade, the justifications given by the Christian preachers for enslaving Africans, and the bigotry that was taught in the sanctuaries of America for four centuries. White was right and whites were the preferred race of the god of the Christians, even the image of the white Jesus glistening in the sunlight, hung over the baptisteries of the churches represented the "ideal" of a god with no blackness anywhere near the purity and sanctity of this pristine whiteness. It is almost impossible for one growing up with such images and such indoctrination to repudiate the inherent racism that comes with race based exceptionalism. "God is white, Jesus is white, white is good, and white presidents are the only ones who should be president," goes the rhetoric. Consequently, Barack Obama, seeking to become the President of the United States in 2008 was seen by some whites as the "anti-Christ" and once he was elected they saw him as the devil who would destroy America. In a study reported in the *Journal of Experimental Psychology* (Volume 46, Issue 5, September 2010, pp. 863-866) Tom Pyszczynski, et. al., demonstrated that it was more likely that respondents would believe that Obama was the anti-Christ if racial priming identified him as African American. In fact, candidates running for election who may have held similar ideas as Obama would not have been considered anti-Christ if they were primed as white candidates. The idea that Obama's blackness had something to do with the degree to which whites accepted the notion that he was anti-Christ, something they would not do with a white candidate, showed descent to a level of racism that would otherwise not appear if the candidate was considered white.

CHAPTER SEVEN

The Haunting Image of Meanness

The Obama Administration of the nation brought out the vilest and meanest spirit one could imagine in a democratic nation against its highest elected official. What is quite remarkable for me is the fact that those who have hounded the president because of his race have neither shame nor guilt. Or if they have either one or the other they have been adept at hiding all sense of morality.

A period in American history that might have been considered one of the brightest moments in human political history where a Speaker of the House and the First African American President made a public peace and created the conditions of unity of people and government passed in rancor, dispute, and with a speaker whose career will become a mere footnote in Congressional history when he could have become a great partner for a just society. . Alas, this was not to be. At one point in his second administration the word was that Obama was too good to be true, too innocent, too nice, too polite to be president; this meant to some of his enemies that he was not fit to be president or was so smart that he had manipulated the press and the social media to protect his image. In fact some people actually believed that because Obama was black it meant that the first election was prejudiced. In an article called "Rhetorical racism: The futility of polling prejudice this election" Tara Wall, who claims that her hate mail says that she is not black enough, wrote (*Washington Times*, September 23, , 2013, A. 23), "Black Americans, it seems, are the one and only ethnic group that must be treated special in polls. Whether it is a poll about religion (which almost never include black evangelicals) or one about racism, it appears as if blacks are the only group in America that is discriminated against. And every issue that arises in the black community–including a run for president–has to have some element of racism or discrimination attached to it."

Wall exuded a simplistic pride when she stated "There is a black man on the ballot for president of the United States for the first time in history. He is running against a white man, with a slight lead and has a pretty good shot at winning. What does that say about racism in America? A lot more than we're giving the American (mostly white) people credit for." Wall assumed that Obama would win with a white majority although she did not explicitly say as much. Wall was wrong on her analysis and wrong on giving white people credit for an election in which the majority of them did not vote for the president. They neither did that during the first nor the second campaign. The percentage of whites that voted for Barack Obama never reached the percentage of black, Hispanics, and Asians voting for him. Yet he refused both an archaeology of bleakness or a rhetoric of bombast making him "inscrutable" to most of the ruffians serving as pundits.

The Tea Party became a force in the Republican Party with the election of Barack Obama. The Tea Party expressed its objections to the President's policies in vile and obscene terms. It was easy for the Tea Party to be plastered with the charge of racism since at their rallies they would often have signage depicting the president as a witch doctor, a monkey, or resorting to calling the president someone who was planning for "white slavery." An occasionally they likened the Congress to a slave owner and the "taxpayer to a "n----r." They were the angriest white people in the land because they could not come to terms with a black president. Some people even threatened to leave the country and move to Canada or Australia.

Professor Christopher Parker of the Wiser Institute for the Study of Ethnicity, Race and Sexuality at the University of Washington conducted a survey that produced some interesting attitudes of Tea Party sympathizers. "The data suggest that people who are Tea Party supporters have a higher probability"—25 percent, to be exact—"of being racially resentful than those who are not Tea Party supporters." Parker said that his data suggested that the attitudes were not just about government but also about race.

Surveyors asked people to respond to a series of questions that are typically used to measure racial hostility. The results were that Tea Party backers expressed more racial resentment than the rest of the population. When read the statement by surveyors that "if blacks would only try harder, they could be just as well off as whites," 73 percent of the movement's supporters agreed, while only 33 percent of people who disapproved of the Tea Party agreed. "Asked if blacks should work their way up "without special favors," as the Irish, Italians, and other groups did, 88 percent of supporters agreed, compared to 56 percent of opponents. The study revealed that Tea Party enthusiasts were also more likely to have negative opinions of Latinos and immigrants." Obviously there appeared to be a correlation between one's conservative credentials as represented by the Tea Party and one's attitude toward race when it came to politics and social mobility.

Obama had mean-spirited enemies throughout the first and the second administration. In fact, Mayor Dean Grose sent a racist Obama watermelon email and was asked to step down from office in 2009; this happened during Obama's first year. Grose came under severe criticism when as Mayor of Los Alamitos he sent the email depicting the planting of watermelons on the lawn of the White House. The caption read "No Easter egg hunt this year."

Keyanus Price, a black businesswoman, received the email and demanded an apology from the Mayor. She told thec Associated Press that "I honestly don't even understand where he was coming from, sending this to me. As a black person receiving something like this from the city-freakin'-mayor–come on."

Grose confirmed that he sent the email to Price and said he was unaware of the racial stereotype that black people like watermelons. He served on the same community youth board with Price. Grose said he sent an apology to the businesswoman and left a voice message apology. "Now I am like–wow, is this really how he feels?" Price said. Los Alamitos is a small town in the traditionally Republican Orange County of California.

A post on Alternet on September 20, 2009 stated that there were 10 "horrifying racist attacks" on Obama. The staff of the website called 2009 the "summer of hate." But the ten horrifying racist attacks underscored the meanness of the attackers. One could almost refer to the entire period of Obama's presidency as a season of hate where crude, thuggish and hateful white conservatives sought to string up the president in every conceivable manner. They tried to and often did frustrate his legislative agenda that was really about saving the nation, especially its economic, physical, and structural health. The legislators railed against the stimulus plan and attacked him for introducing health care, and would not allow an overhaul of the nation's bridges, roads, and rails.

I think that what we were seeing with the elite white response was the loss of what can only be described as a tribal inheritance of white Americans. They knew that something was being lost with the election of President Obama.

When Glenn Beck organized a Washington March supported by the Tea Parties, the faithful came with signs portraying Obama as an African "witch" doctor, with a bone through his nose, and signs saying that the President was President of Kenya.

I have always respected the way that former President Jimmy Carter carried himself in and out of office and his statement about the Obama noise was that the actions against him showed "intensely demonstrated animosity" toward Obama and that it was based on the fact that he was a black man (*Guardian*, September 19, 2009). In fact, the *Guardian* said, "The former president said racism had come to the surface across the country because of a belief held by many whites that an African American is not qualified to be in the White House."

To underscore their idea that Obama was not qualified to be President some of the pundits wrote and said horrible things about Obama, always couching their language in the whispers of racists. For example, former House Whip, Representative Roy Blunt, R-Mo, made a statement to his conservative colleagues about British colonists complaining in India about monkeys stealing the balls from the golf course. "So for this golf course, and this golf course only, they passed a rule, and the rule was, you have to play the ball where the monkey throws it." Rush Limbaugh rushed to say that food-safety people would soon go after Oreo cookies. "Might have to put that off until Obama's out of office, but they'll eventually go after Oreos" a soft reference to those who are black on the outside and white on the inside. Both Beck and Limbaugh thought out loud that Obama was "using health reform to force reparations for slavery from white America" and that the health care bill was an attempt to place the African Americans in charge of white people."

Other whites shaken by the fact that a black man would want to run for the Presidency and the fact that he actually won depicted him as an animal. The racist depiction of Obama as a skunk or any animal shows neither regard for the man nor the office of President. One cartoonist portrayed the President as an "ape". Another person went so far as to attack First Lady Michelle Obama.

Raven Symone sat in as a co-host on ABC News' "The View" after Rodner Figueroa a TV host for Univision lost his job for saying that Michelle Obama looked like a character from *Planet of the Apes*.

Rosie Perez, a panelist on the program, was outraged by Symone's defense of the remarks and was infuriated by the statements about the First Lady.

Figueroa later wrote to the First Lady stating, "I want to clarify that I'm not racist and in no way was my comment directed at you, but rather the work of the [makeup] artist, which left much to be desired."

Figueroa was apparently shocked by the Filipino makeup artist's transformation of the First Lady "Mind you, you know that Michelle Obama looks like she's part of the cast of 'Planet of the Apes,' the film," he said.

Univision fired Figueroa, and pulled references to him from their websites. In a statement to the Huffington Post, Univision called Figueroa's remarks "completely reprehensible and in no way reflect the values or opinions of Univision."

He went on to assert that he'd "been an activist for causes in favor of minorities. He also said he'd "been discriminated against" in the past because he is gay.

During the exchange on "The View," Perez suggested that Figueroa's offensive remarks were in-line with some cultural norms in Latin America. This was obviously a stretch for a defense despite the fact that certain racist attitudes did exist in South America and the Caribbean.

Symone ended her defense of the questionable remarks with the peculiar statement:

> "But some people look like animals. Is that rude? I look like a bird… so can I be mad at somebody that calls me 'Toucan Sam?'"

The attack on the American First Lady seemed particularly rude and ignorant, but there were other assaults that were just as bad.

In December 2011 a Tea Party group in Kansas depicted the President as a skunk and then went on to say that it was satire not racism because "the skunk is half black, half white, and almost everything it does stinks." The *Hutchinson News* reported that the local NAACP president Darrell Pope saw no humor in the depiction. The group's webmaster, Thomas Hymer, told the *The Hutchinson News* the statement was just political satire. Later police in Connecticut found two dead skunks on a telephone pole that had a sign attached reading "Obama Stinks." It appears that someone got the hot idea to use the two-colored skunk as an apt portrayal of the President. The idea that everything he does stinks is a direct insult to the President.

Interestingly, the skunk depiction in Hutchinson, Kansas, had much more to do with human relations. It was later used as a legal exhibit in a wrongful termination lawsuit in 2013, two years later, when Lukas Lucas claimed that he was the victim of racial discrimination. According to Lucas, Mile Meldman, a wealthy Los Angeles real estate developer sent him the racist email that Meldman claimed came from someone else with the caption: "The skunk has replaced the eagle as the new symbol of the American presidency. It is half black, half white, and everything it does stinks." The ad is evidence of the currency of racist imagery and racist attitudes in an era when the word is postracialism or postracism. This is not a class attack; it is something meant to portray the President in a negative light. Reaching for an animal image the creators of the ad found the skunk to be a symbol of their own repulsion of something black and white. (http://www.bet.com/news/politics/2013/11/19/racist-attack-on-obama-gets-cameo-in-a-wrongful-termination-suit.html).

But perhaps one of the meanest portrayals meant to prevent any possible thought of Obama as a great president appeared on the infamous George Zimmerman's Twitter site. Soon after deranged reporter Vestal Flanagan shot two white reporters in Roanoke, Virginia on August 26, 2015, Zimmerman began a series of racist rants on his Twitter account. In one he referred to President Obama as an "Ignorant Baboon." However, apparently Zimmerman was provoked because he claimed Obama did not respond to the black reporter killing the two white reporters, although Obama did respond to the shooting, but not as quickly as Zimmerman wanted him to respond.

Zimmerman's anger boils over and spills out as he tweeted the photo on the next page.

Of course, Zimmerman is neither a historian nor apparently is he a good student of contemporary politics; he is a vigilante killer of a teenage black male. Obama's record will be judged and evaluated by those who are interested in defining his administration's legacy on the basis of what he set out to do and what he did.

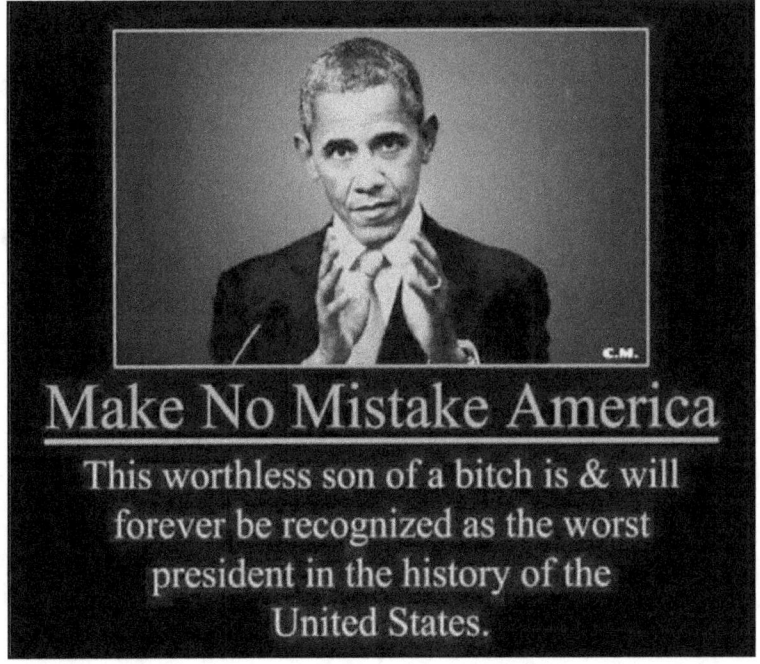

Perhaps one of the most constant themes was the assault on the physical image of Michelle Obama. Here more than anywhere else the Right Wing sought to appeal to the basest of their racial fears. The idea that a black woman who was physically very fit, muscularly toned, shaped like many typically beautiful black women, would be the First Lady of the country so infuriated the anti-Obama crowd that some of them called the First Lady a man or an ape. Clearly the reaction of meanness was rooted in the lack of understanding of humanity, human societies, cultures, and the realities of black is beautiful although I would think that most of the people attacking Michelle were born in America. What this means is that after Africans have lived in this country longer than many who claim to be white Americans there is still little appreciation or understanding of the African idea of beauty. Michelle, in the eyes of most black Americans and some whites, is a gorgeously beautiful woman with the kind of essential grace and strength that constitutes elegance.

It would be wrong to assume that the only critics of the President are conservatives. It is better to say that only the extreme Right-Wing uses the kind of mean-spirited invective against the person of the President that I have been reporting on. Liberals, on the other hand, from Cornel West to Ted Rall, and others have questioned certain policies of the President. I have strong opinions, and have voiced them, about the Africa policy of the Obama government. I do not know how his advisors could have advised him to

Negative ads about the President of the United States.

open up to Cuba and not to Zimbabwe. Why do we have sanctions on Zimbabwe? I worked in Zimbabwe and have returned to the country twice and I cannot see the reason for the sanctions and for the lack of embrace to the Zimbabwean people. The policy is a hang-over from the ancient regimes of the Republicans who hated Robert Mugabe for making his people free and proud by taking back the land that had been stolen from their ancestors. I did not like the Libyan policy and have spoken on it because it was wrong headed, counter-productive, and meant to set African unity back by many years. Gaddafi had faults but he was far away not the worst person American leaders deal with on a daily basis. While Cornel West and Maulana Karenga have more domestic reasons for opposing certain Presidential policies, I take the position that how the President thinks about the entire African project is important. On the other hand, Ted Rall, a veteran political cartoonist, has been quite critical of President Barack Obama for other reasons. He is concerned that the President has not been progressive enough.

"They'll have to find someone else to write the next stimulus bill," it read, prompting concerns that the paper was using a long-standing racist slur to smear the President.

Hikes in floods of obscene and vulgar responses about President Obama were seen in both the first and second term elections. Bigoted commentaries and sneers crowded the Internet and political rallies as the attacks on Obama reached the highest intensity ever seen in presidential elections. Racial slurs yelled in

This New York Post cartoon depicts police shooting an ape.
(Wednesday 18 February 2009)

angry voices accompanied white rallies in Mississippi, Alabama, and Louisiana.

According to the Southern Poverty Law Center "America's number of race-hate fringe groups soared after Obama's election in 2008. Ever since, their publications and Web sites have spewed contemptuous slurs about Obama, as well as all U.S. minorities." As Ralph Ellison noted in his 1970 essay, "What America Would Be Like Without Blacks," "Despite his racial difference and social status, something indisputably American about Negroes not only raised doubts about the white man's value system, but aroused the troubling suspicion that whatever else the true American is, he is also somehow black."

The Haunting Image of Meanness

History will record that the first visibly US President of African origin presided over some of the most important changes in American society. Among the accomplishments of Obama's administration include the passing of the health care law, getting the stimulus bill passed to rescue the American economy, regulated Wall Street by re-organizing the financial sector, ended the war in Iraq, eliminated Osama Bin Laden who was responsible for the World Trade and Pentagon attacks, saved the American auto industry, recapitalized banks, started withdrawing troops from Afghanistan, opened the door to Cuba, the longest US war, reversed President Bush's torture policy, acted on immigration by Executive Order that was later overturned by the court, began a pivot to Asia, upgraded America's response to climate change, got rid of "Don't ask, Don't tell" for gay soldiers, used the extent of his executive powers to close the gun loopholes, realigned the drug oppression penalties among prisoners, and began actions to close Guantanamo. I am certain that others can create different lists but this one speaks to the achievements of a President without much support from Congress.

Future historians will recall the compelling times that created a President ready for action as soon as he took charge of the Office of the President in 2009. The downturn in the economy caused partly by the billions of dollars spent for wars without taxation and exuberant financial dealings that made a housing bubble burst challenged Barack Obama even before he took the office and when the time came he had to act. There are many reasons progressives and liberals can criticize the President but one of those reasons cannot be because he is black. On the other hand, as we have shown, the Right-Wing was principally concerned that Barack Obama was not one of them, did not look like them, did not act like them, and was not like anyone that the extreme Far Right votarists knew. Their verbal lynching of Obama was from the start based on race and their reactions to his legislative proposals were also based on their desire to defeat the President that their votes could not conquer. He stood in his place unmoved by the resentments and recklessness of a virtual mob of bigots.

www.ingramcontent.com/pod-product-compliance
Lightning Source LLC
Chambersburg PA
CBHW050555300426
44112CB00013B/1932